CULTURE

CULTURE

LIVING AS CITIZENS OF HEAVEN ON EARTH—
COLLECTED INSIGHTS FROM

A. W. TOZER

MOODY PUBLISHERS
CHICAGO

© 2016
THE MOODY BIBLE INSTITUTE
OF CHICAGO

All Scripture quotations are taken from the King James Version.

Interior and cover design: Erik M. Peterson
Cover art by Unhidden Media, unhiddenmedia.com

Library of Congress Cataloging-in-Publication Data

Names: Tozer, A. W. (Aiden Wilson), 1897-1963, author.
Title: Culture : living as citizens of heaven on earth / A.W. Tozer.
Description: Chicago : Moody Publishers, 2016.
Identifiers: LCCN 2016015943 (print) | LCCN 2016016499 (ebook) | ISBN
  9781600668012 | ISBN 9781600669040 ()
Subjects: LCSH: Christian life. | Christianity and culture.
Classification: LCC BV4501.3 .T69725 2016 (print) | LCC BV4501.3 (ebook) |
  DDC 248.4--dc23
LC record available at https://lccn.loc.gov/2016015943

We hope you enjoy this book from Moody Publishers. Our goal is to provide high-quality, thought-provoking books and products that connect truth to your real needs and challenges. For more information on other books and products written and produced from a biblical perspective, go to www.moodypublishers.com or write to:

Moody Publishers
820 N. LaSalle Boulevard
Chicago, IL 60610

3 5 7 9 10 8 6 4

Printed in the United States of America

CONTENTS

Publisher's Note		7
1.	The Sacrament of Living	9
2.	An Unchanging Book in an Ever-Changing World	19
3.	Two Portraits of the Church	29
4.	The Great Test: Modifying the Truth	39
5.	A Biblical Concept of the Church	51
6.	A Model Church	63
7.	Integration or Repudiation?	75
8.	Sure! Pay That Income Tax	79
9.	Measuring Spirituality by Public Prayers	83
10.	Wanted: Courage with Moderation	85
11.	The Honest Use of Religious Words	91
12.	The Right Attitude toward Our Spiritual Leaders	95
13.	The "Spiritual-or-Secular" Tightrope	99
14.	This World: Playground or Battleground?	115
15.	Are We Evangelicals Social Climbing?	119
16.	Why the World Cannot Receive	123
17.	Affirmation and Denial	135
18.	Resisting the Enemy	139
19.	The Wind in Our Face	143
20.	The Cross Does Interfere	147
21.	Power Requires Separation	151
22.	Science and Philosophy More Bigoted Than Religion	155
23.	Nothing Can Destroy Christianity If We Live Like Christians	159
24.	We Are What We Are Anyway	163
	Sources	165

PUBLISHER'S NOTE

Like the men of Issachar, A. W. Tozer was a man who understood his times and who knew what to do. The twenty-four selections that follow are a small sampling of Tozer's writings on what it means to be a Christian in a world that is largely uninterested in Christ.

He covers topics like truth, the meaning of the church, the veracity of Scripture, and how Christians should live in this world while maintaining their identities as citizens of another.

Tozer wrote with conviction and purpose. He held nothing back in his challenge to his fellow Christians on how to live as Christ did:

We who call ourselves Christians are supposed to be a people apart. We claim to have repudiated the wisdom of this world and adopted the wisdom of the cross as the guide of our lives. We have thrown in our lot with that One who while He lived on earth was the most unadjusted of the sons of men. He would not be integrated into society. He stood above it and condemned it by withdrawing from it even while dying for it. Die for it He would, but surrender to it He would not. (excerpted from chapter 7)

While these are merely the words of one servant of the Lord, from many decades ago, they also represent timeless truths that ought to be heeded in our day. The context may change and the specific battles may vary, but the truth remains the same.

THE SACRAMENT OF LIVING

Whether therefore ye eat, or drink,
or whatsoever ye do, do all to the glory of God.

1 CORINTHIANS 10:31

One of the greatest hindrances to internal peace that the Christian encounters is the common habit of dividing our lives into two areas—the sacred and the secular. As these areas are conceived to exist apart from each other and to be morally and spiritually incompatible, and as we are compelled by the necessities of living to be always crossing back and forth from the one to the other, our inner lives tend to break up so that we live a divided instead of a unified life.

Our trouble springs from the fact that we who follow Christ inhabit at once two worlds—the spiritual and the natural. As children of Adam we live our lives on earth subject to the limitations of the flesh and the weaknesses and ills to which human nature is heir. Merely to live among men requires of us years of hard toil and much care and attention to the things of this world. In sharp contrast to this is our life in the Spirit. There we enjoy another and higher kind of life—we are children of God; we possess heavenly status and enjoy intimate fellowship with Christ.

This tends to divide our total life into two departments. We come unconsciously to recognize two sets of actions. The first are performed with a feeling of satisfaction and a firm assurance that they are pleasing to God. These are the sacred acts and they are usually thought to be prayer, Bible reading, hymn singing, church attendance, and such other acts as spring directly from faith. They may be known by the fact that they have no direct relation to this world, and would have no meaning whatever except as faith shows us another world, "an house not made with hands, eternal in the heavens" (2 Corinthians 5:1).

Over against these sacred acts are the secular ones. They include all of the ordinary activities of life that we share with the sons and daughters of Adam: eating, sleeping, working, looking after the needs of the body, and performing our dull and prosaic duties here on earth. These we often do reluctantly and with many misgivings, often apologizing to God for what we consider a waste of time and strength. The upshot of this is that we are uneasy most of the time. We go about our common tasks with a feeling of deep frustration, telling ourselves pensively that there's a better day coming when we shall slough off this earthly shell and be bothered no more with the affairs of this world.

This is the old sacred-secular antithesis. Most Christians are caught in its trap. They cannot get a satisfactory adjustment between the claims of the two worlds. They try to walk the tightrope between two kingdoms and they find no peace in either. Their strength is reduced, their outlook confused, and their joy taken from them.

I believe this state of affairs to be wholly unnecessary. We have gotten ourselves on the horns of a dilemma, true enough, but the dilemma is not real. It is a creature of misunderstanding. The sacred-secular antithesis has no foundation in the New Testament. Without doubt, a more perfect understanding of Christian truth will deliver us from it.

The Lord Jesus Christ Himself is our perfect example, and He knew no divided life. In the presence of His Father He lived on earth without strain from babyhood to His death on the cross. God accepted the offering of His total life, and made no distinction between act and act. "I do always those things that please him," was His brief summary of His own life as it related to the Father (John 8:29). As He moved among men, He was poised and restful. What pressure and suffering He endured grew out of His position as the world's sin bearer; they were never the result of moral uncertainty or spiritual maladjustment.

Paul's exhortation to "do all to the glory of God" is more than pious idealism. It is an integral part of the sacred revelation and is to be accepted as the very Word of Truth. It opens before us the possibility of making every act of our lives contribute to the glory of God. Lest we should be too timid to include everything, Paul mentions specifically eating and drinking. This humble privilege we share with the beasts that perish. If these lowly animal acts can be so performed as to honor God, then it becomes difficult to conceive of one that cannot.

That monkish hatred of the body, which figures so prominently in the works of certain early devotional writers, is wholly without support in the Word of God. Common modesty is found in the sacred Scriptures, it is true, but never prudery or a false sense of shame. The New Testament accepts as a matter of course that in His incarnation our Lord took upon Him a real human body, and no effort is made to steer around the downright implications of such a fact. He lived in that body here among men and never once performed a non-sacred act. His presence in human flesh sweeps away forever the evil notion that there is about the human body something innately offensive to the Deity. God created our bodies, and we do not offend Him by placing the responsibility where it belongs. He is not ashamed of the work of His own hands.

Perversion, misuse, and abuse of our human powers should give us cause enough to be ashamed. Bodily acts done in sin and contrary to nature can never honor God. Wherever the human will introduces moral evil we have no longer our innocent and harmless powers as God made them; we have instead an abused and twisted thing, which can never bring glory to its Creator.

Let us, however, assume that perversion and abuse are not present. Let us think of a Christian believer in whose life the twin wonders of repentance and the new birth have been wrought. He is now living according to the will of God as he understands it from the written Word. Of such a one it may be said that every act of his life is or can be as truly sacred as prayer or baptism or the Lord's Supper. To say this is not to bring all acts down to one dead level; it is rather to lift every act up into a living kingdom and turn the whole life into a sacrament.

If a sacrament is an external expression of an inward grace, then we need not hesitate to accept the above thesis. By one act of consecration of our total selves to God we can make every subsequent act express that consecration. We need no more be ashamed of our body—the fleshly servant that carries us through life—than Jesus was of the humble beast upon which He rode into Jerusalem. "The Lord hath need of [him]" (Matthew 21:3) may well apply to our mortal bodies. If Christ dwells in us, we may bear about the Lord of glory as the little beast did of old and give occasion to the multitudes to cry, "Hosanna in the highest."

That we *see* this truth is not enough. If we would escape from the toils of the sacred-secular dilemma, the truth must "run in our blood" and condition the complex of our thoughts. We must practice living to the glory of God, actually and determinedly. By meditation upon this truth, by talking it over with God often in our prayers, by recalling it to our minds frequently as we move about among men, a sense of its wondrous meaning will take hold of us. The old painful duality will go down before a restful unity of life. The knowledge that we are all God's, that He has received all and rejected nothing, will unify our inner lives and make everything sacred to us.

This is not quite all. Long-held habits do not die easily. It will take intelligent thought and a great deal of reverent prayer to escape completely from the sacred-secular psychology. For instance, it may be difficult for the average Christian to get hold of the idea that his daily labors can be performed as acts of worship acceptable to God by Jesus Christ. The old antithesis will crop up in the back of his head sometimes to disturb his peace of mind. Nor will that old serpent, the devil, take all this lying down. He will be there in the cab or at the desk or in the field to remind the Christian that he is giving the better part of his day to the things of this world and allotting to his religious duties only a trifling portion of his time. And unless great care is taken, this will create confusion and bring discouragement and heaviness of heart.

We can meet this successfully only by the exercise of an aggressive faith. We must offer all our acts to God and believe that He accepts them. Then hold firmly to that position and keep insisting that every act of every hour of the day and night be included in the transaction. Keep reminding God in our times of private prayer that we mean every act for His glory; then supplement those times by a thousand thought-prayers as we go about the job of living. Let us practice the fine art of making every work a priestly ministration. Let us believe that God is in all our simple deeds and learn to find Him there.

A concomitant of the error which we have been discussing is the sacred-secular antithesis as applied to places. It is little short of astonishing that we can read the New Testament and still believe in the inherent sacredness of some places. This error is so widespread that one feels all alone when he tries to combat it. It has acted as a kind of dye to color the thinking of religious persons and has colored the eyes as well so that it is all but impossible to detect its fallacy. In the face of every New Testament teaching to the contrary, it has been said and sung throughout the centuries and accepted as a part of the Christian message, that which it most surely is not. Only the Quakers, so far as my knowledge goes, have had the perception to see the error and the courage to expose it.

Here are the facts as I see them. For four hundred years Israel had dwelt in Egypt, surrounded by the crassest idolatry. By the hand of Moses they were brought out at last and started toward the land of promise. The very idea of holiness had been lost to them. To correct this, God began at the bottom. He localized Himself in the cloud and fire, and later when the tabernacle had been built He dwelt in fiery manifestation in the Holy of Holies. By innumerable distinctions God taught Israel the difference between holy and unholy. There were holy days, holy vessels, holy garments. There were washings, sacrifices, offerings of many kinds. By these means, Israel learned that *God is holy*. It was this that He was teaching them, not the holiness of things or places. The holiness of Jehovah was the lesson they must learn.

Then came the great day when Christ appeared. Immediately He began to say, "Ye have heard that it was said by them of old time . . . but I say unto you" (Matthew 5:21–22). The Old Testament schooling was over. When Christ died on the cross, the veil of the temple was rent from top to bottom. The Holy of Holies was opened to everyone who would enter in faith. Christ's words were remembered, "The hour cometh, when ye shall neither in this mountain, nor yet at Jerusalem, worship the Father. . . . But the hour cometh, and now is, when the true worshippers shall worship the Father in spirit and in truth: for the Father seeketh such to worship him. God is a Spirit: and they that worship him must worship him in spirit and in truth" (John 4:21, 23–24).

Shortly after, Paul took up the cry of liberty and declared all meats clean, every day holy, all places sacred, and every act acceptable to God. The sacredness of times and places, a half-light necessary to the education of the race, passed away before the full sun of spiritual worship.

The essential spirituality of worship remained the possession of the church until it was slowly lost with the passing of the years. Then the natural *legality* of the fallen hearts of men began to introduce the old distinctions. The church came to observe again days and seasons and times. Certain places were chosen and marked out as holy in a special sense. Differences were observed between one and another day or place or person. The "sacraments" were first two, then three, then four, until with the triumph of Romanism they were fixed at seven.

In all charity, and with no desire to reflect unkindly upon any Christian, however misled, I would point out that the Roman Catholic Church represents today the sacred-secular heresy carried to its logical conclusion. Its deadliest effect is the complete cleavage it introduces between religion and life. Its teachers attempt to avoid this snare by many footnotes and multitudinous explanations, but the mind's instinct for logic is too strong. In practical living, the cleavage is a fact.

From this bondage reformers and puritans and mystics have labored to free us. Today, the trend in conservative circles is back toward that bondage again. It is said that a horse, after it has been led out of a burning building, will sometimes, by a strange obstinacy, break loose from its rescuer and dash back into the building again to perish in the flame. By some such stubborn tendency toward error, fundamentalism in our day is moving back toward spiritual slavery. The observation of days and times is becoming more and more prominent among us. "Lent" and "holy week" and "good" Friday are words heard more and more frequently upon the lips of gospel Christians. We do not know when we are well off.

In order that I may be understood and not be misunderstood, I would throw into relief the practical implications of the teaching for which I have been arguing, i.e., the sacramental quality of everyday living. Over against its positive meanings, I should like to point out a few things it does not mean.

It does not mean, for instance, that everything we do is of equal importance with everything else we do or may do. One act of a good man's life may differ widely from another in importance. Paul's sewing of tents was not equal to his writing of an epistle to the Romans, but both were accepted of God and both were true acts of worship. Certainly it is more important to lead a soul to Christ than to plant a garden, but the planting of the garden *can* be as holy an act as the winning of a soul.

Again, it does not mean that every man is as useful as every other man. Gifts differ in the body of Christ. A Billy Bray is not to be compared with a Luther or a Wesley for sheer usefulness to the church and to the world; but the service of the less gifted brother is as pure as that of the more gifted, and God accepts both with equal pleasure.

The "layman" need never think of his humbler task as being inferior to that of his minister. Let every man abide in the calling wherein he is called, and his work will be as sacred as the work of the ministry. It is not what a man does that determines whether his work is sacred or secular, it is why he does it. The motive is everything. Let a man sanctify the Lord God in his heart and he can thereafter do no common act. All he does is good and acceptable to God through Jesus Christ. For such a man, living itself will be a priestly ministration. As he performs his never-so-simple task, he will hear the voice of the seraphim saying, "Holy, holy, holy, is the LORD of hosts: the whole earth is full of his glory" (Isaiah 6:3).

Lord, I would trust Thee completely; I would be altogether Thine; I would exalt Thee above all. I desire that I may feel no sense of possessing anything outside of Thee. I want constantly to be aware of Thy overshadowing presence and to hear Thy speaking voice. I long to live in restful sincerity of heart. I want to live so fully in the Spirit that all my thoughts may be as sweet incense ascending to Thee and every act of my life may be an act of worship. Therefore I pray in the words of Thy great servant of old, "I beseech Thee so for to cleanse the intent of mine heart with the unspeakable gift of Thy grace, that I may perfectly love Thee and worthily praise Thee." And all this I confidently believe Thou wilt grant me through the merits of Jesus Christ Thy Son. Amen.

AN UNCHANGING BOOK IN AN EVER-CHANGING WORLD

Then he answered and spake unto me, saying, This is the word of the Lord unto Zerubbabel, saying, Not by might, nor by power, but by my spirit, saith the Lord of hosts.

ZECHARIAH 4:6

One area of thinking that needs reform is our practical beliefs about God's design for mankind. I emphasize *practical* beliefs, because there is a difference between nominal beliefs and practical ones. A nominal belief is what you hold in name, and the practical belief is what you hold in reality and what holds you. While probably there are not many faults to be found with the nominal beliefs, there are a great deal to be found with the practical beliefs. These practical beliefs need restoration to their happy and bright state with faults and abuses purged.

It has been a long time since Jesus was born in Bethlehem,

died on the cross, rose again the third day, ascended to the right hand of God the Father Almighty, and sent the Holy Spirit to establish His church. Since those days there have been changes in the world so radical, sweeping, all-pervading, and revolutionary as to be entirely incredible to anybody living in Jesus' day.

RESTORATION TO BELIEF IN THE TRUTH

Today's world was entirely unimaginable to the people of those times. Have these changes forced God to modify His plans for His church and for mankind? Here is where we have fallen by the wayside. Here is where we need a reformation, a purgation, a removal of the faults, and a restoration again of the faith of Christians to a belief in the truth.

Many Christians say, without a question, "Yes, that is true." Actually, I suppose they would not like to have it put to them like that: people do not like the most realistic constructions. What would the liberals and modernists say if you backed them in a corner with the question, "Do you think God has been forced to change His mind?" I do not think anybody would quite have the courage to say yes. Nevertheless, they do say it little by little until they have brainwashed their people.

In effect, they say that the Bible must be interpreted in the light of new developments. A book that was written in the day when people rode donkeys must be reinterpreted to mesh with contemporary society. They say that the prophets and apostles mistook what God intended to do. The Bible is outmoded and largely irrelevant. *Irrelevant* means that it is not related to anything. *Outmoded* means we have new modes of thinking and living now, so the Bible is out-of-date—a back-issue magazine. We must, therefore, reassess its teachings and rethink our beliefs and hopes.

I am not overstating this at all. This is what is being taught today. It gets into the newspapers, and people are saying that the Bible must be interpreted in the light of all these changes. The apostles and prophets were mistaken. They had ideas that were good and advanced for their day, but not advanced for our day. We know more about ourselves, human motivation, and the nature of things than they did back then. Therefore a book written when people thought the earth was flat and the sun rose in the morning, crossed over the earth, and went down into the sea cannot possibly be taken seriously. While it certainly contains some beautiful poetry and some marvelously inspiring thoughts about human nature and the world in which we live, nevertheless all this is to be understood and reinterpreted, reassessed and rethought.

I challenge the idea that we are advanced. I know the majority of modern educators, newspaper writers, TV personalities, radio reporters, politicians, and all the rest do not agree with me. Nevertheless, I challenge the idea that we are any further advanced than they were in the days of Jesus.

If we are so advanced, then I want to ask some questions. Why do we kill thousands of human beings each year with automobiles? Because we ride automobiles instead of donkeys, we are advanced? If we are so advanced in our day, why are the penitentiaries packed full and the mental hospitals crowded? If we are so advanced, why is the whole world a powder keg? If we are so advanced, how is it that we have weapons that can annihilate the world? If we are so advanced, why is it that people cannot walk alone in the parks anymore? Why is it that workers who get out at midnight never walk home alone anymore? Why is it in this advanced age that drugs, violence, abortion, and divorce are soaring?

There is a mindset that thinks every motion is progress. Every time you move you are progressing. Then there is the mindset that thinks whenever you move in a straight line you are going forward, forgetting that you can move in a straight line and be going backward.

THE TRAGEDY OF THE CENTURY

The tragedy of the century is that Protestants have accepted this as progress and actually believe it. The children of the protesters, children of the Reformation, have been brainwashed and indoctrinated by those who believe that changes have made a difference in God's plan, a difference in Christianity, and a difference in Christ. We have been brainwashed to believe that we cannot read the Bible as we used to. We must now read it through glasses colored by change. We have been hypnotized by the serpent, the devil, into believing that we no longer have a trustworthy Bible, so Protestantism is no longer a moral force in the world.

Protestantism is not a force in this world because we have sold out to the brainwashers. Instead of being the sons and daughters of the protesters, we are now yes-men and yes-women. Running our Protestant world are people who talk solemnly about Christ but who do not mean what the Bible means. They talk about revelation and inspiration, but they do not mean what our fathers meant.

The second prominent tragedy is that the gospel churches are confused and intimidated by numbers. They accept the belief that there has been change and that Christians must adjust to the change. The word used is *adjustment.* We must get adjusted, forgetting that the world has always been blessed by the people who were not adjusted. The poor people who get adjusted cannot do much anyhow. They are not worth having around.

In every field of human endeavor progress has been made by those who stood up and said, "I will not adjust to the world." The classical composers, poets and architects were people who would not adjust. Today society insists that if you do not adjust you will get a complex. If you do not get adjusted, you will have to go to a psychiatrist.

JESUS WAS MALADJUSTED

Jesus was among the most maladjusted people in His generation. He never pretended to adjust to the world. He came to die for the world and to call the world to Himself, and the adjustment had to be on the other side.

The contemporary world is a result of radical changes down the generations amounting to revolution: the scientific revolution, the industrial revolution, the communications revolution, the philosophical revolution, and the social revolution. Are we going to accept the belief that the Bible must be interpreted anew in the light of these developments? Are we going to allow ourselves to accept the doctrine that the prophets and apostles were mistaken about God? Are we going to allow society to tell us that the Bible is outmoded and largely irrelevant and must therefore be reassessed in the light of modern advancements?

Has God changed? Are we going to accept it? Is there a change in the purpose of God? Have the changes in human society startled or shocked God?

Must we, in order to remain intellectually respectable and have good standing with these who doubt the Word, humbly say, "Well, I do not believe in miracles"? Or have we got enough of our Protestant protest and courage to stand up and say, "I believe in miracles whenever God Almighty wants to perform them. I believe that whenever God wants to do anything that is out of the ordinary and contrary to or at least above the common processes of nature, He is able to do it. I believe the miracles of Jesus Christ were real miracles. I believe the miracles of the Old Testament were real miracles." Are we going to allow ourselves to be brainwashed along with all the rest?

Or are we going to dare to stand and protest and be known over this country as being Protestants indeed? We would be people who refuse to adjust but who make the world adjust to us.

When you adjust, you are dead. The same is true if a church adjusts to these ideas. If you adjust, you are done. But if you dare to stand, the world will adjust to you. I can promise you that. Not all will adjust to you, but at least some will.

Some have asked themselves, "Is communism the unforeseen and unpredicted invasion? Is that what God did not know about, what Christ did not foresee?" Has Christ, after having come down the centuries triumphant, at last met His Waterloo? What is your answer to that? My answer is a loud, roaring, resounding no! He has never met His Waterloo and He never will. He, the Lord Christ, is going to ride the sky on a white horse, and upon His thigh will be written, "KING OF KINGS, AND LORD OF LORDS" (Revelation 19:16). The rich men, the mighty men, the scientists, the doctors, and the lords of finance will cry for the rocks and the mountains to fall on them, to hide them from the wrath of the Lamb and the fury of His power.

Have God's people at last been plucked out of His hand? He said we would never be plucked out of His hand, but did He know enough to tell us that? Have there been some new advancements and developments that He did not foresee? The answer again is no!

SHALL WE SURRENDER?

Shall we surrender to the world? No! Shall we surrender to liberalism? No! Shall we surrender to apostate Protestantism? The answer is no! Shall we surrender to the brainwashed churches whose preachers are afraid to stand up and talk as I am? The answer again is no!

Our church is going to go the way of the gospel. We are not radicals nor fools. We do not fast forty days. We dress like other people, drive vehicles, and have modern homes. We are human and like to laugh. But we believe that God Almighty has not changed and that Jesus Christ is the same. He is victorious, and we do not have to apologize for Him. We do not have to modify, adjust, edit, or amend. He stands as the glorious Lord, and nobody needs to apologize for Him.

If our answer to the questions I have asked is yes, then we

leave to our children a heritage of nothing but death. I say now, shall we believe the ringing words, "For I am the LORD, I change not" (Malachi 3:6)? I believe them. Shall we believe that "Jesus Christ the same yesterday, and to day, and for ever" (Hebrews 13:8)? I do. We must believe the words that say, "To him that overcometh will I give to eat of the tree of life, which is in the midst of the paradise of God" (Revelation 2:7). "He that overcometh shall not be hurt of the second death" (2:11). "To him that overcometh will I grant to sit with me in my throne" (3:21).

We are not going to be sheep running over the precipice because other dumb sheep are running over it. We see the precipice—we know it is there. We are listening to the voice of the shepherd, not the voice of terrified sheep. The terrified, intimidated sheep are going everywhere.

I stand solidly and protest this. I believe we need a reformation back to the belief that God knew what He was talking about in the first place. We need to get back to the belief that Jesus Christ did not miss anything but foresaw it all, back to the belief that the apostles spoke as they were moved by the Holy Spirit. We must return to the belief that our fathers who gave us the great creeds were not fools but wise saints who knew what they were talking about. We must get back to the belief that Protestants are to protest, dissenters are to dissent, and nonconformists must refuse to conform.

HOW THE COVENANTERS STOOD

Read history and see how the covenanters stood and died rather than give up to the enemy. Are we satisfied to be degenerate sons of great fathers? Consider A. B. Simpson who walked the shores of the Atlantic Ocean with cardboard in the soles of his shoes because he did not have money to buy new ones. He prayed and groaned in spirit and cried to God for people of all nations who had not heard the gospel. He prayed, "Oh, God, I believe Jesus Christ thy Son is the same yesterday, today and forever." We are his descendants, but we ought to spend a day in sackcloth and ashes.

At thirty-six, Simpson was a Presbyterian preacher so sick that he said, "I feel I could fall into the grave when I have a funeral." He could not preach for months at a time because of his sickness. He went to a little camp meeting in the woods and heard a quartet sing, "No man can work like Jesus/ No man can work like Him." Simpson went off among the pine trees with that ringing in his heart: "Nobody can work like Jesus; nothing is too hard for Jesus. No man can work like Him." The learned, stiff-necked Presbyterian threw himself down upon the pine needles and said, "If Jesus Christ is what they said He was in the song, heal me." The Lord healed him, and he lived to be seventy-six years old. Simpson founded a society that is now one of the largest evangelical denominations in the world, The Christian and Missionary Alliance.

We are his descendants and we sing his songs. But are we going to allow ourselves to listen to that which will modify our faith, practices, and beliefs, water down our gospel and dilute the power of the Holy Spirit? I, for one, am not!

I am cheered to know so many of you are with me on this. We are going to go to the New Testament and be Bible Christians. We are going to sell out to God and not the devil. We are going to pray more, read our Bibles more, and attend prayer meeting more. We are going to give more and break bad habits by the power of God. We are going to become Christians after God's heart. We are going to be protesters in an hour when the smooth, sickly, slippery, rotten, backslidden, degenerate, apostate Christianity is accepted. We are going to stand for God, to act like simple Protestant Christians, to act like our Presbyterian Scottish forebears, to act like our English Methodist forebears, to act like the dear old Baptist who broke the ice in the creek and baptized people in the freezing water. They had a saying in those days, "Nobody ever caught a cold getting baptized in the ice." God Almighty saw to it that nobody ever died of pneumonia.

Those Protestant forebears made these two nations, the United States and Canada. They made this continent. Are we going to be descendants of which they should be ashamed? Or are we going to say, "Lead on, we are following. You followed Jesus Christ, and we are following you."

John Thomas was a dear old Welsh preacher I used to hear. While he preached he would raise his hands and say, "You supply the grit and God will supply the grace." He was right. You've got the grit; God has the grace.

TWO PORTRAITS OF THE CHURCH

*Then he answered and spake unto me, saying, This is the
word of the Lord unto Zerubbabel, saying, Not by might,
nor by power, but by my spirit, saith the Lord of hosts.*

ZECHARIAH 4:6

On our farm in Pennsylvania there were cherry trees, which
were attacked by little parasites of some sort. A parasite
would get into a little branch, pierce the bark, and exude a gum.
Then the branch would get a knot on it and bend. All over the
trees were those little bent places with gummy knots. After two
or three years, those cherry trees would not bloom. If they did,
the blooms usually dropped early and the cherries did not come
to fruition. If the blooms did not drop early, the cherries would
be flat and undeveloped or only red on one side.

My father was not too interested in fruit. He was interested in
cattle, horses, and grain. If my father had known how he could
have protected those trees before they got into that wretched

condition and properly sprayed or treated them, he could have gotten rid of the worms and bugs and saved the trees and fruit.

I believe that a pastor who is content with a vineyard that is not at its best is not a good husbandman. It is my prayer that we may be a healthy and fruitful vineyard and that we may be an honor to the Well Beloved, Jesus Christ the Lord, that He might go before the Father and say, "These are mine for whom I pray, and they have heard the Word and have believed on Me." (See John 17:6–10.) I pray that we might fit into the high priestly prayer of John 17, that we would be a church after Christ's own heart so that in us He might see the travail of His soul and be satisfied.

In order for us to be a vine like that, there must be basic purity. Each one must have a great purity of heart. I believe that there are no emotional experiences that do not rest upon great purity of heart. No one can impress me or interest me in any kind of spiritual manipulation if his or her heart is not pure— even if it is raising the dead. Sound righteousness in conduct must be at the root of all valid spiritual experience.

A NEW WAVE OF RELIGION

I am afraid of a new wave of religion that has come. It started in the United States, and it is spreading. It is a sort of esoteric affair of the soul or the mind, and there are strange phenomena that attend it. I am afraid of anything that does not require purity of heart on the part of individuals and righteousness of conduct in life.

I also long in the tender mercies of Christ that among us there may be the following:

1. *A beautiful simplicity.* I am wary of the artificialness and complexities of religion. I would like to see simplicity. Our Lord Jesus was one of the simplest men who ever lived. You could not involve Him in anything formal. He said what He had to say as beautifully and as naturally as a bird sings on the bough in the morning. That is what I would like to see restored to the churches. The opposite of that is artificiality and complexity.

2. *A radiant Christian love.* I want to see a restoration of a radiant Christian love so it will be impossible to find anyone who will speak unkindly or uncharitably about another or to another. This is carefully thought out and carefully prayed through. The devil would have a spasm. He would be so chagrined that he would sulk in his self-made hell for years. There should be a group of Christians with radiant love in this last worn-out dying period of the Christian dispensation, a people so loving that you could not get them to speak unkindly and you could not get them to speak uncharitably.

3. *A feeling of humble reverence.* I am disappointed that we come to church without a sense of God or a feeling of humble reverence. There are false religions, strange religious cults, and Christian cults that think they have God in a box someplace, and when they approach that box they feel a sense of awe. Of course, you and I want to be saved from all paganism and false cultism. But we would also like to see a company of people who were so sure that God was with them, not in a box or in a biscuit, but in their midst. They would know that Jesus Christ was truly

among them to a point that they would have a sense of humble reverence when they gathered together.

4. *An air of joyous informality.* The great English preacher who was pastor for many years of Westminster Chapel in London, G. Campbell Morgan, left his church and went down to Wales where the Welsh revival was going on under Evan Roberts earlier in this century. He stayed there awhile and soaked up the glory of it. I read the sermon that he preached to his congregation afterward, and it was as near to scolding as that great preacher ever got. He said to them, "Your singing is joyless, your demeanor is joyless, and you do not have the lift or joy that I saw in Wales." He urged them that they might get into a place where that sense of joyous informality might be upon them.

5. *A place where each esteems others better than himself or herself.* As a result of that, everyone should be willing to serve, but nobody would be jockeying for position. Nothing is quite so bitterly humorous as ambition in the church of Christ. It would be as though a man who was on a lifeboat being saved from certain salty death in the ocean depths should become ambitious to become captain of the little boat on its way to save those on board. It is as though a man were to enter a disaster area where an earthquake had hit and people were dying and would fight for a high position there.

NO PLACE FOR THE AMBITIOUS OR LAZY

The church of Christ is no place for the ambitious or the lazy. I would like to see our Christian communion be a place where each one esteems the other better than himself or herself. For that reason, nobody should push and nobody should jockey for position. On the other hand, nobody should refuse to serve.

6. *A childlike candor.* I love children because of their unbelievably beautiful candor. They look at you and say the most utterly simple things. If they were just a little older they would blush to the roots of their hair, but they are utterly and completely candid. I like to talk with them and have them come up and chat with me because they are bound to tell me things before they leave. If you do not want it told, do not tell the little ones because they just tell anything. They do not have anything to hide. I believe that with the limitations proper to our adult years we ought to be at a place where spiritually we should be so candid there would be no duplicity, no dishonesty.

A duplex is a house where there is more than one dwelling; there are two dwellings. Duplicity is the same thing—it means two. Judas Iscariot, for instance, was duplicity incarnated. He was so slick that even the disciples did not know which one was the traitor. They said, "Lord, is it I?" (Matthew 26:22). And Jesus said, "He that dippeth his hand with me in the dish, the same shall betray me" (26:23). He had to tell them. This son of perdition had lived with Jesus and His eleven disciples for three years and had fooled them so completely that they did not know which one was the traitor when the showdown came. They had to have a little sign to indicate. That was the slickest piece of duplicity I know about. He was two-faced, and he could change faces with the occasion. He was so slick in the change that nobody caught on. He showed one face to Jesus and His disciples and the other to the enemies of Jesus. Now that is duplicity.

A PEOPLE WITHOUT DUPLICITY

In Christian communion we ought to be a people without duplicity. Each one of us has only one face. I know that if you have more than one face to present to the public, something is desperately wrong. One of your faces is going to fall under an awful judgment of God.

We must be without duplicity, dishonesty, and hypocrisy. What is hypocrisy? Hypocrisy is an old Greek word used for an actor on stage, somebody who pretended to be what he or she was not. He was not Job but he pretended to be Job, so he put on a mask of some sort and strutted around the stage. People do it today, too. They get up on the theater stage or on TV, glue whiskers on, and put on makeup to become people they are not. A hypocrite is an actor, somebody who is playing a part.

7. *A presence of Christ that is as the fragrance of myrrh and aloes.* When you become accustomed to the smell of His garments, you will be spoiled for anything less. If we never smell the myrrh and aloes out of the ivory palaces, we may go along a lifetime and not miss it. But one beautiful whiff of the fragrance of these garments and we will never be satisfied with anything less.

When my wife and I were first married, we attended a church of The Christian and Missionary Alliance in Akron, Ohio. There was something on that church, a sense of the fragrance of God. The great Dr. Gerow preached there in those days. The church had some sweet Christian brethren, some wonderful men and women of God, and there was a fragrance on that place. I have never forgotten it. I was between nineteen and twenty-one for the three years I spent in that church, and I do not remember getting help from others of my age. But how I remember getting help that is with me to this day from the older saints whose garments were fragrant with the myrrh, aloes and cassia out of the ivory palaces!

8. *Answers to prayer; miracles should not be uncommon.* I am not a miracle preacher. I have been in churches where they announced miracle meetings. If you look in the Saturday newspaper you will see occasionally somebody who will hit town and announce, "Come out and see some miracles." That kind of performing I do not care for.

You cannot get miracles as you would get a chemical reaction. You cannot get a miracle as you get a wonderful act on stage by a magician. God does not sell Himself into the hands of religious magicians. I do not believe in that kind of miracles. I believe in the kind of miracles that God gives to His people who live so close to Him that answers to prayer are common and these miracles are not uncommon.

John Wesley never lowered himself to preach miracles once in his life. But the miracles that followed John Wesley's ministry were unbelievable. On one instance he had to make an engagement, and his horse fell lame and could not travel. Wesley got down on his knees beside his horse and prayed for its healing. Then he got back up and rode, without the horse limping, to where he was going. He did not publicize the miracle and say, "We'll have a big tent here and advertise it." God just did those things for him.

While C. H. Spurgeon did not preach healing, he had more people delivered in answer to his prayer than any doctor in London. Those are the kinds of miracles I am talking about.

In light of the Scripture, in light of the judgment seat of Christ, and in light of eternity, is what I am asking unreasonable?

Is the description I have given unreasonable? Is this portrait of a true church an unreasonable portrait? Is it undesirable and impossible that we should have this kind of church? Is this an unscriptural picture?

The church should be a healthy, fruitful vineyard that will bring honor to Christ, a church after Christ's own heart where He can look at the travail of His soul and be satisfied. Among the people should be a beautiful simplicity and a radiant Christian love so it would be impossible to find gossips and talebearers. There should be a feeling of humble reverence and an air of joyous informality, where each one esteems others better than himself or herself, where everyone is willing to serve but no one jockeys to serve. Childlike candor without duplicity or dishonesty should mark the church, and the presence of Christ should be felt and the fragrance of His garments smelled by His beloved. Prayers should be answered so regularly that we think nothing of it. It would be common because God is God, and we are His people. When necessary, miracles would not be uncommon.

Is that, in the light of Scripture, unreasonable and undesirable to expect of a church? Is there something better? If there is something better, you name it!

Is this impossible? Is anything impossible with God? Is anything impossible where the Lord Jesus Christ is? Is this unscriptural? No! The only thing that is unscriptural about this vision is that it is not up to the standard of Scripture yet. The scriptural standards are still high.

If you answer, "No, it is not unreasonable, undesirable, or impossible," then you are saying you believe in this. If you believe in this, if you would like to become the church that could begin this reformation, this change toward the better, this recapturing of the ancient power of God in the souls of people, then there must be a radical psychological break with the prevailing religious mood.

I have told you by careful description what a church ought to be. Now I am going to describe churches as they are, with beautiful exceptions, of course. There are pure saints in almost all the churches, a few here and there, but the prevailing religious mood is self-centered instead of world-centered. Instead of being outgoing and soul-winning, the average church is self-centered and self-satisfied. We make our reports and we spend pages telling what wonderful good boys and nice girls we have been. Self-satisfaction seems to be upon us all.

Worldliness of spirit is the prevailing mood in the average church, along with carnality of heart. To the Corinthians, Paul said in effect, "You are carnal and I cannot speak to you of spiritual matters. I would like to come to preach deep things to you, but you are too carnal."

Another prevailing mood of the average church is to be Christian in name but in practice to be unchristian. Our trouble is not that we refuse to believe right doctrine, but we refuse to practice it. We have the peculiar contradiction of believing the right thing and living the wrong way, a strange anomaly within the church everywhere.

In the church many are lovers of pleasure more than lovers of God. If you do not like what I am saying, I want to ask you something. Think about the company you run with. What do they talk about most? God and the love of God, or other things? You decide that.

Many Christians today will not endure sound doctrine. Paul described these people as having "itching ears" (2 Timothy 4:3). They did not like sound doctrine, but they were Christians. They called themselves Christians, but their ears were itchy.

A commentator I read some years back explained this. In Paul's day the pigs had a disease called "itching ears." The symptom was that their ears got inflamed and itched terribly. The only way they could get relief from these inflamed ears was to go to a pile of rocks and rub their ears earnestly and vigorously. The stones scratched their ears for the time being.

Paul saw that, smiled a sad smile, and said, "I am running into Christians here and there who are just like that. They love pleasure more than God and will not endure sound doctrine. They have itching ears so they will be eager for something else beside the sound doctrine and holy ways. They will pile up teachers everywhere and rub their ears for dear life." That is a most dramatic and colorful illustration. A lot of so-called Christians have to have piles of rocks to rub their ears. They will not endure sound doctrine. I think that is a description of the churches, Protestant and evangelical.

In the light of New Testament predictions, teachings, and standards, is what I just said about the prevailing religious mood untrue? Is what I have said about the prevailing religious mood uncharitable? Is it extreme? I do not think it is, but I only ask you to do one thing: Look around you and look in your own heart. See which of these pictures describes the churches you know.

THE GREAT TEST: MODIFYING THE TRUTH

There is a great decision that every denomination has to make sometime in the development of its history. Every church also has to make it either at its beginning or a little later—usually a little later. Eventually every board is faced with the decision and has to keep making it, not by one great decision made once for all, but by a series of little decisions adding up to one great big one. Every pastor has to face it and keep renewing his decision on his knees before God. Finally, every church member, every evangelist, every Christian has to make this decision. It is a matter of judgment upon that denomination, that church, that board, that pastor, that leader and upon their descendants and spiritual children.

The question is this: *Shall we modify the truth in doctrine or practice to gain more adherents?* Or shall we preserve the truth in doctrine and practice and take the consequences? If the decision is that we modify the truth and practice of the church, then we are responsible for the consequences, whatever they may be. God already knows what the consequences are, and history has shown what they are. But if we choose to preserve the truth, then God accepts the responsibility.

Businesspeople have to make that choice in business. Everyone has to make it at income tax time. Students have to make it in school. We have to make it everywhere in our lives as we touch society. Shall we preserve the truth and the practice of the truth, or shall we alter it just comfortably in order to be more popular, gain more adherents, and get along easier in the world?

Actually such a question should never need to be asked. It is like asking, "Should a man be faithful to his wife?" There is only one answer to that question. When we ask, "Shall we preserve the truth and practice of the church, or shall we modify it for immediate and visible results?" we ought to have only one answer. It is not a debatable question, and yet it is one that has to be constantly debated in the secret prayer chamber. It is constantly debated when conferences meet, when boards meet, and when a pastor must make a decision.

A commitment to preserving the truth and practice of the church is what separates me from a great many people who are perhaps far greater than I am in ability. This is my conviction, long held and deeply confirmed by a knowledge of the fact that modern gospel churches, almost without exception, have decided to modify the truth and practice a little in order to have more adherents and get along better. When we make a decision to modify the truth, we bring the consequences of that choice upon ourselves. What have the consequences been?

One has been an absence of a spirit of worship in the church. Many people do not even know what is meant by a spirit of worship. That is tragic. I wish God would either change things a little or give me a sight of His glory among His people. I admit that sometimes I feel like the man of God who said,

> *And I said, Oh that I had wings like a dove! for then would I fly away, and be at rest. Lo, then would I wander far off, and remain in the wilderness. Selah.* (Psalm 55:6–7)

Many of the Lord's people do not know what you mean when you mention a spirit of worship in the church. They are poor victims of boards, churches, denominations, and pastors who have made the noble decision to modify the truth and practice a little. But God responded, "If you do, I will withdraw from you the spirit of worship. I will remove your candlestick."

ABSENCE OF SPIRITUAL DESIRE

A second consequence is the absence of spiritual desire. How many people do you know who are all burnt up with spiritual desire and longing after God? How many have tears of eagerness in their eyes when you talk to them? How many say, "Oh, that I might know God better!" Our fathers had spiritual desire, and they spent days with God.

Another result is coldness of heart, which is similar to an absence of spiritual desire. Once you have been baptized with the fire of inward longing, you will never be satisfied with coldness of heart.

G. Campbell Morgan, the great English preacher, went to Wales to see the Welsh revival and then came back to Westminster Chapel. What he saw in Wales so moved the great expositor that he got up and roundly lectured his audience. In effect he said, "You are a cold bunch. You don't even sing warmly; you don't even sing right." Morgan had heard the Welsh sing—they sang the Psalms and nothing else. A man would get up to preach, and in the audience somebody would raise a psalm and off the whole congregation would go, singing a psalm. The preacher would have to sit down in confusion. God had never told him to preach anyhow, and he knew it. Then two or three people would get down on their knees and get converted—no altar calls; they just got converted where they were. The fire of God would fall upon them everywhere.

One man got up and said, "I have a sermon tonight that consists of three Cs," and he listed his three points, each beginning with the letter C. Before he was halfway through the first C, the Holy Spirit fell on the audience. Somebody with a high voice raised a psalm, and they sang him down. He sat down with the other two Cs unmolested. Those people had warmth of heart. But we do not have it because we have made the ignoble decision that we would rather compromise a little bit on truth and practice.

LACK OF SPIRIT OF PRAYER

A fourth consequence is the lack of the spirit of prayer. No child is born until there is labor. When Evan Roberts, whom God used to start the great Welsh revival, was in a prayer meeting somebody said to him, "Evan, never miss a prayer meeting,

THE GREAT TEST: MODIFYING THE TRUTH

because the one you miss may be the one when the Holy Spirit falls." So Evan never missed a prayer meeting. One night when he was on his knees the Holy Spirit fell upon him, and he began to pray, "Oh, God, bend me, bend me, bend me." Another man was praying, and Evan did not want to break in. Roberts described the experience, "I waited for the other man to get through, but it seemed he would never get through; he prayed on and on. Finally, he tapered off and petered out and said, 'Amen.'" Evan began to pray, and the place was shaken with his prayer. From there on the revival in Wales was underway.

Now that is the spirit of prayer. When the spirit of prayer falls on people, God answers their prayer and things are done. When a spirit of prayer is not on us, we just mumble on endlessly. But when the spirit of prayer is on us, the Spirit praying in us to the God above us will get things done around us.

NO SENSE OF GOD'S PRESENCE

A fifth consequence of modifying the truth is that there is no sense of God's presence in the average church. I get around quite a bit, but I do not go into many places where I find the sense of God's presence. There are almost no answers to prayer and almost no divine manifestations. This leads to the deadliest consequence of all: the absence of saintliness.

There are a few saints around who are so sold out to God that you could not keep them still. They are always coming up with something, and you know that they have been in the presence of the Lord. They live their faith regularly and consistently. Everything they do is congruous with everything they testify to.

43

The spirit of worship should be on us until tears are as common as the snow over Toronto. It is the will of God that we should be burnt with spiritual desire. We should be singing, "Oh, Jesus, Jesus, dearest Lord, forgive me if I say, for very love Thy precious name a thousand times a day." We would not be singing hypocritically—we would mean it.

It is God's will that we should have no coldness of heart. The difference between coldness of heart and warmth of heart is the difference between being in love and not being in love. When a person loves deeply, whether someone of the opposite sex or a baby or a child, it warms the affections. Sometimes our telephone rings at night, and the operator at the other end of the line says, "Would you receive this phone call, please, collect from somebody named Becky?" As soon as that call comes from my daughter, I feel something warm inside. I get calls from people for whom I do not feel anything warm. Somebody usually wants me to do something. I like those people, but I am not particularly warm. That is the difference between coldness and warmth of heart.

God wants us to have warm hearts, and He wants us to have a spirit of prayer so prayer is effective. Most prayer is like forever turning a key on a dead battery, and the starter does not even whine. Turn the key for twenty minutes saying, "Our Lord and our Father . . ." twenty-nine times, and there is still not a buzz. God does not want us to pray like that. He wants a spirit of prayer to be on the people. You can have that spirit of prayer. He wants to answer your prayer, and He wants the sense of His presence to be upon you. Always remember one thing: when the Spirit of the Lord comes, that is the presence, and you have that presence. God does want to manifest Himself.

Our eagerness to be proper, never get out of order, and never have anything fanatical happen continues until nothing happens at all. There is no divine manifestation, and there is an absence of saintliness. Yet God wants us to know His presence and exhibit saintliness.

USUALLY FOLLOW A TREND

How did we get into this fix that we are in? Well, evangelicals usually follow a trend. It is dangerous to follow a trend unless your eyes are open and you know where the trend is going. This trend began in the last decades of the last century and carried on with some big names promoting it. In their zeal to make converts and adherents, they oversimplified the Christian faith. That is our difficulty today. We oversimplify it, and yet we never get simple. Isn't that odd? We oversimplify the truth, and yet we have the most complex, mixed-up beliefs.

The average Christian is like a kitten that has found a ball of yarn and has played with the yarn and romped until it is wrapped in a cocoon. The kitten cannot get itself out. It just lies there and whimpers. Somebody has to come unwind it. We have tried to be simple, but instead of being simple we have simplified—we have not become simple. We are sophisticated and overly complex.

We have simplified so Christianity amounts to this: God is love; Jesus died for you; believe, accept, be jolly, have fun, and tell others. And away we go—that is the Christianity of our day. I would not give a plug nickel for the whole business of it. Once in a while God has a poor bleeding sheep that manages to live on that kind of thing and we wonder how.

I have traveled through the American Southwest, and I have seen swaybacked cattle. You could count every rib if the train was not going too fast. They stand out there between stalks of long grass, brown and dry and hard. As we sailed by on a fast, streamlined train, I wondered how the poor things ever live. Somehow or other they manage to do it.

You will find a few of God's people here and there even in that kind of atmosphere. Whole generations of Christians have grown up believing that this is the faith of our fathers living still, in spite of dungeons, fire, and sword. The devil would not be caught dead trying to kill anybody for acting like that. It does not bother him—the only thing the devil hates is somebody who is after him.

When my friend Alan Redpath shakes your hand to say goodbye, he smiles and says, "Well, K.O.K.T.D." That stands for "keep on kicking the devil." The devil does not mind if you are not a bother to him, and most of us are not. The devil looks at us, smiles, and says, "That poor little emaciated weakling can't do my kingdom any harm." A whole generation has thought this to be Christianity. That is the faith of our fathers, living still, in spite of dungeon, fire, and sword. Nobody ever put people like that in a dungeon—they are already there. They were born into it. Nobody ever threw them to the flames, because they are harmless.

There must come a reformation, a revival that will result in a fresh emphasis on neglected truth. I do not preach any new truth. I do not have a new doctrine, and if anybody would come here preaching a new doctrine, I would say, "I'm sorry, but we already have our doctrine." I would not allow that preacher in the pulpit. We do not want new doctrine—we want fresh emphasis on doctrine already well known by all of us.

REVIVAL THAT WILL MEAN PURITY OF HEART

We must have a revival that will mean purity of heart as a normal standard for everybody. We must be clean people, and not only clean outside. Average evangelicals do not smoke, and because they do not, they feel they are doing God's service. Thank God they do not smoke—that is a start toward clean living. But purity of heart goes deeper.

Purity of heart is taken for granted, yet we must have it to be clean people. Even in my lifetime—and I have not lived five hundred years yet—I can well remember that when people lost their tempers they had to go to an altar and get cleansed. People knew they were out of victory and were not right with God. People were supposed to have a pure heart. We need and must have a revival that will mean divine energy to give our Christian witness power.

"But ye shall receive power, after that the Holy Ghost is come upon you: and ye shall be witnesses unto me" (Acts 1:8). It is frustrating to talk to people about the Lord and not get anywhere at all, to not have any power at all.

In addition to becoming people with clean hearts, we must become a fellowship where there are frequent answers to prayer and the calling out of Christian missionaries and preachers. I would like to see our young people feel the call of God on them until they have to leave us and begin preaching. I would like to see the Spirit of God move upon us until our young people cannot afford to sit and figure out who they are going to marry and when. That will come in its time, but they will be thinking, *Where can I serve God?* Then one day, suddenly, the hand of God will be laid on their shoulders and off they will go. How many young people like that have I seen? Many young people do come to me and say, "I feel that God has His hand on me."

A man I knew during World War II was something of an odd-ball in temperament. I never thought he would amount to very much. He went off to the war, was wounded, and was tumbling over a cliff. He would have fallen to his death below. Before he went over he said, "I am called to Ethiopia." As he was tumbling and sliding slowly toward certain death, he knew he was called to Ethiopia. A great big old tough sergeant saw him, grabbed him as he was going over, and hauled him back, and he recovered. He came back after the war but nobody wanted him; he did not have the proper schooling. Finally, a well-known missionary society sent him to Ethiopia. He went over there and has been preaching there ever since.

WE NEED REVIVAL AND REFORMATION

I believe we desperately need revival and reformation to come. In Exodus they came to the end of four hundred years of Israel's defeat. I read of Hezekiah, the son of an evil father, Ahaz, who had brought Israel to the lowest moral condition that it had been in for a long time. Ahaz died and his son Hezekiah reigned in his stead. Hezekiah was a holy man and sought God immediately. He threw the dirt out of the temple and sent word throughout all Israel and said, "Come to the meeting." Israel began to be blessed. They cleansed the temple and started the fires again. (See 2 Chronicles 29.) The first thing they knew, they had a revival on their hands. It was also Hezekiah who prayed when Sennacherib came down like a wolf on a foal with his cohorts all gleaming in purple and gold. It was under Hezekiah that the breath of the Lord smote those thousands and delivered Jerusalem. (See 2 Chronicles 32:1–23.)

When the Israelites returned from Babylon, God spoke to a man who cared, a man with a concern, who was cupbearer to the king. The king said, "What's the matter with you? You haven't been gloomy like this before." Nehemiah responded, "Your majesty, pardon me, please, but I can't help it. My heart is broken. My father's city is in rubble and the foxes run over the walls. The glorious temple where we used to worship Jehovah has been razed to the ground and the religion of Israel is gone into decay." King Artaxerxes, not knowing that God was working in his life, said, "You go back to rebuild Jerusalem." That was the beginning of the return from Babylon.

Since Bible times we have had these periods of refreshing from the presence of the Lord. I just happened to notice a comment in a book I was reading today on this subject. The writer said, "God added a postscript to that." Here it is: "He that hath an ear, let him hear what the Spirit saith unto the churches; To him that overcometh will I give to eat of the tree of life, which is in the midst of the paradise of God" (Revelation 2:7).

Everyone has a private battle going on, a private fight. You are in the midst of a wicked and adulterous generation, but you have got to overcome. He who overcame indicates that you also can overcome, but He indicates that not all do. You can overcome your own flesh, which will be the hardest. You can overcome tradition and custom, which will be the second hardest. You can overcome all things. "To him that overcometh will I give to eat of the tree of life, which is in the midst of the paradise of God" (2:7).

The world is waiting to hear an authentic voice, a voice from God—not an echo of what others are doing and saying, but an authentic voice.

A BIBLICAL CONCEPT
OF THE CHURCH

Around the beginning of World War I we had a visitation in the United States, not of spiritual power, but of what I have named *tabernacleism.* Anyone with a good personality and preaching ability would start a tabernacle around the corner, get a crowd, pull out of the churches, and proceed to poke fun at the churches. I can understand why there was such a revolt—the churches were pretty dead. A lot of money was spent to build these tabernacles, but often the men who founded them left town and nobody else could keep them up, so the crowds wandered away. The mortgage holders foreclosed, and the tabernacles were left high and dry.

The depression killed the movement. Nobody had any money, so it did not pay to go around starting churches. As a result, however, today we have immense church buildings throughout the United States. They are not good for anything, but they left behind a residue—a bad and dangerous philosophy. This philosophy is actually a dangerous theology regarding the church. The church was thrown out and said to be of no account—come when you please, go when you must; hold no creed but Christ, no law but love, no pastor but Jesus, no membership, no anything. This philosophy has left us high and dry like a shore after a storm when the wind has blown.

It is time for us to reconsider this matter of the church. Most people think of the church as a familiar social fact. Their attitude toward Protestantism generally is that of a matter of course, and people, even average Christians, think they are in favor of the church. They favor the church much the same as they support motherhood, decency, and sanitation. It is as accepted as a convention that we never question or doubt. If anybody does question or doubt, they are considered communists or atheists. People will even pour out their money to support social convention.

But I wonder how many ever sit down and say, "What is this? Maybe the church is just something that is here; it doesn't have any value and doesn't have any reason for being here." How many present-day Christians have ever searched the Scripture with a serious burden on their hearts to know what the church is? Is it simply a convention that is carried on? How many Christians have ever prayed earnestly for light from heaven about it?

It seems that the average person spends more time and intellectual labor each year filling out income tax forms than he or she spends in a lifetime trying to learn from the Scriptures and from the light of the Spirit what the church is and what he or she ought to do about it. Why is it in the world? What did Jesus mean when He said, "Upon this rock I will build my church; and the gates of hell shall not prevail against it" (Matthew 16:18b)? If people were to chew their pencils and walk the floor and go out for a walk and come back and work on it and search and think and discern and divide and go through all that they have to go through to make out their income taxes every year, I believe that they could come up with some wonderful answers.

MUST UNDERSTAND THE UNIVERSAL CHURCH

When we know what the universal church is, we will understand what a local church is. The average local church is to a large extent a social organization where well-intentioned people get together and know each other. They are drawn together by coffee, tea, friendship, skating parties, and things like that. Those things are harmless. But when we know what the church really is, we will understand that while these things are all right on the margin of the church, they are not the purpose of it.

Meeting, shaking hands, and drinking coffee are perfectly legitimate if we do not need them—they are not what holds us together. But when those activities are what hold us together, we do not have a church; we have something else. Unfortunately, we might as well admit it: that is often all that the churches have.

First we have to have a philosophy about the church. What is the church? I want to use three illustrations to show what the true Church of Jesus Christ is.

THE BRIDE OF CHRIST

First, the church is the bride of Christ. Jesus was a complete man. He had all the nature of a man, but He never married. He could have, but He never did. He never married any woman though He was a true and complete man. He never married a daughter of a woman that He might marry His whole church, the bride.

A true local church is the bride of Christ in recapitulation, in miniature. Everything that is in the whole church of Christ should be recapitulated in the local church. The church, part of it in heaven and part of it on earth, is the bride of Christ. Our Lord Jesus washed His bride, regenerated her, and prepared her. He is coming back to take her—the whole church—as His bride.

But any local church is the whole church in recapitulation, just as a local election recapitulates a national one. The same liberty is expressed. The same candidates run. They talk about each other; they plead their own worth and put up bulletins and do the same thing on a small scale that they do on the federal level. That may be a poor illustration, but the whole bride of Christ is recapitulated. Any local church is what the whole church is, just in miniature.

Husbands, love your wives, even as Christ also loved the church, and gave himself for it; That he might sanctify and cleanse it with the washing of water by the word, That he might present it to himself a glorious church, not having spot, or wrinkle, or any such thing; but that it should be holy and without blemish. So ought men to love their wives as their own bodies. He that loveth his wife loveth himself. For no man ever yet hated his own flesh; but nourisheth and cherisheth it, even as the Lord the church. (Ephesians 5:25–29)

This figure drawn from husbands and wives is applied directly without apology to Jesus Christ and His church. Just as a young man would not marry a dirty bride, so Jesus Christ will not marry a church that has stains or wrinkles or blemishes. His desire is for a glorious church, and He wants to love that church as a man loves his own bride.

There was a man named Adam, and he was the first bachelor. God told Adam to call in all the animals and name them. According to the Bible, names were given after the nature of the animals. Adam named the bear after the bear nature and the lion after the lion nature. Then the Bible makes this touching comment—"But for Adam there was not found an help meet for him" (Genesis 2:20). Some people think that just means there was no woman yet. But what it means is that God and Adam had not found any nature like Adam's yet. Adam had to have someone who was satisfactory for him. No one was worthy of him. There had to be somebody with his nature. There was no one appropriate because the rest were the beasts of the field and the fowls of the air—they did not have the same nature as Adam, who was made in the image of God.

God told Adam to lie down. Adam obeyed and went into a deep sleep. There in a state of deep anesthesia, God operated on the man and took from his chest a rib. God then fashioned the rib into a woman, gave her life, and called her woman—the life-giver, who shall give life to all the race. When Adam came out of his sleep, he looked around and saw Eve. She looked good in his sight. Adam knew Eve, she conceived a son, and thus the race began.

But then there was another Adam. First Corinthians 15 tells us about a second Adam, the last Adam, Jesus Christ the Lord. He had a nature that was divine. He was divine, God in flesh. Jesus was a perfect and complete man, but He married no daughter of woman. He married no daughter of woman because there was none found worthy of Him.

Just as He had done with Adam, God put Jesus on the cross in a deep sleep and opened His side. Out from His side flowed not a rib but water and blood. From that water and blood God is washing, cleansing, and preparing a bride worthy of Jesus.

God did not create Eve from nothing as He had Adam, but He created her from the wounded side of Adam. Even so, the Lord is not creating a race that does not now exist to be His church. He takes the race that now exists—certain members of it—and washes it in the blood that came from the wounded side. By the Holy Spirit, He gives the nature of Christ to the bride, so she will be worthy of Him.

There was not among the daughters of Eve one that was appropriate and satisfactory for Jesus. Therefore He is preparing Himself a bride who has His nature, as Eve had the nature of the husband out of whose side she came. A theologian once noted that God took the bone that made the woman not from Adam's head, that she might lord it over him; not from his feet, that he might lord it over her; but from his heart, that she might understand him, and he might love her. That is what the church is—the bride of Christ.

If you are a member of the true church of Christ, then you are a member of the company that will make up the true bride of Christ. As a local church, we are a miniature of the bride of Christ.

THE BODY OF CHRIST

A second description of the church is the body of Christ. Jesus Christ is the head, and as the head of His church He directs it. My hands move because my head tells them to. My head directs my body. The head of a local church is not the pastor, but Jesus Christ the Lord. He is the head of the universal church of which the local church is a part. A local church is not all the body of Christ, but in miniature it is the body of Christ.

Third, the church is depicted as an ark on the floodwaters. As the ark of Noah floated on the waters and contained all who would be salvaged, so the church of Jesus Christ is an ark on the flood waters and contains all who will be salvaged. Remember that! All in the ark are saved, and all outside the ark perish. All around us is a perishing world, and we float on top of it in a little ark called the church. All that are not in the church—the ark—will perish.

You say, "Now hold on a minute. Do you mean to say that if you don't join the Avenue Road Church, you will be lost?" No, but what I do say is that the church is the ark containing the ransomed, and inside the ark is life. Outside the living church of Christ are the lost. Inside are the saved. You are not saved by joining a church, which is a mistake local churches make.

The animals all came into Noah's ark by the door. Christ is the door to the church, and whoever will be saved must come in by the door. There is no other ark on the flood. Suppose someone said, "Well, hold on a minute. Don't be so narrow-minded. Let's be tolerant. We do not want to get in Noah's ark; we want an ark of our own." Well, there weren't any other arks on the flood. It was either get into Noah's ark or perish. A few got into Noah's ark, and God preserved the race.

In the church of Christ, God is salvaging a small number from the flood. A fatal error is the independent life—to say that you are a Christian, but you don't associate with any churches. You are a Christian, but you don't feel the necessity to join a church. It is true that there are hypocrites in the church—not in the true church, but in the local assembly. Even Jesus had His Judas. The local assembly and the true church of Christ are sometimes not synonymous.

Sometimes people come into the local church who have never come into the universal church. People join a church who have never been born into the true church. Some churches actually throw the doors open and say, "Now we'll sing the closing hymn for those who want to unite with the church. Come to the front." Al Capone could come in and join. Nobody asks any questions; they just take in anybody. I do not believe in that at all, and I know you do not either.

GET INTO THE
UNIVERSAL CHURCH FIRST

I believe that if you are going to get into a local church, you should first be in the universal church, which Jesus purchased with His own blood. You should get into the church with rebirth, the Holy

Spirit, and regeneration. Then you should join a local assembly. It is impossible to receive Christ and reject His people. How do you find the Shepherd? Go where the sheep are! If you do not know where the Shepherd is, then go where the sheep are. All else being equal, that is where you will find the Shepherd. Whoever receives Christ must receive His people too. Jesus said, "He that receiveth you receiveth me" (Matthew 10:40). Whoever rejects the bride rejects the Bridegroom, and whoever rejects the flock rejects the Shepherd. I think that is clear enough.

Consider this illustration: Two young couples marry in June. One is a Christian couple and takes a serious view of life. Their home is full of love, and they are looking forward to a family. The other two love each other too, in a Hollywood sort of way, and look forward to skin diving, waterskiing, and just having fun. They do not want any children. In the course of time, after two or three years, both of the women have a little baby; one was wanted and one was not.

The Christian parents look at their little baby, their hearts glow, and they say, "Isn't she absolutely wonderful?" This first couple feels a sense of sacredness, and so they pray, plan, and say, "Wasn't God good to give us this little one?" And she becomes a spiritual gift to them. They know that when she grows up she will be like other people with tantrums, but they take her as a gift from God. Bringing up this little baby becomes a sort of sacrament to them.

The other couple have their baby, and of course they love her, but they never quite see it like the other couple. It never occurs to them to pray, and as soon as she is old enough, they send for a babysitter and go on their way. The point is that the first couple understood the sacredness of their baby. The other couple was not thinking of the sacredness of their baby, but rather they were thinking of having fun. They took the baby as a necessary evil that they learned to like after a while.

This illustration also gives you two views of the church. Suppose I do not know what a church is, but I want to come to a church for the social fact and I join it because I think it would be better to join than not. In that case I take the same attitude toward the church as the second couple had toward their baby. The experience does not have the glow of sacredness. But if I see there is a great church being salvaged from the wreckage, just as Noah and his family were salvaged, and the church is found throughout the whole world in local groups, I begin to see the sacredness of the local church.

What a different attitude you will take toward the church! You will say, "How lovely that I ever got in." The church will glow to you and have a sense of sacredness on it. If you find any blemish in the church, you will do what the young Christian couple did with their baby—correct it.

If you want fellowship with the church, if you have not formally joined, there are two ways to do so. One is to pray in public, give money, show enthusiasm, and fill out a card. The other is to do first things first—join the universal church—and then also fill out a card.

PUBLIC CONFESSION

An important part of joining the church is public confession. Why does the Lord want us to make a public confession?

The Bible says,

The word is nigh thee, even in thy mouth, and in thy heart: that is, the word of faith, which we preach; That if thou shalt confess with thy mouth the Lord Jesus, and shalt believe in thine heart that God hath raised him from the dead, thou shalt be saved. For with the heart man believeth unto righteousness; and with the mouth confession is made unto salvation. (Romans 10:8–10)

The heart believes and the mouth confesses. Both are necessary to salvation. Even the thief on the cross made his poor, pitiful confession.

That is why God wants us to fellowship with each other, get together, and tell the world and tell each other—because with the mouth confession is made for salvation. My plea is for those who have never undergone the marvel of the regeneration of new birth to take this seriously. Remember you get into the ark through the door, and Jesus Christ is the door. If you reject the ark, you reject the door, and if you reject the door, you perish in the flood.

MUST BE BORN INTO THE FAMILY

To become a member of the body of Christ and join with the bride of Christ, you must be born into the family of Christ. It happens by believing in your heart that Jesus is Lord and confessing your faith with your mouth to the people. This is reasonable, and I do not understand why anybody should find fault with it.

Suppose you were somewhere in the world, and someone asked you your nationality. Is there anybody here that would be ashamed to say where you were from? Why then should you go through life being secret Christians, too frightened, too scared to say, "I am a Christian"? If Jesus Christ has honored you by finding you and laying His hand on you, you ought never be ashamed of Him. You should be able to stand anywhere at any time and say, "I do not care who knows it. I am a Christian." Be proud.

I want the world to know that I am a Christian. From reading the lives of the saints I know I have a long way to go, and I want you to know that, too! I have a sharp tongue and an abrupt manner, and sometimes I say things that hurt feelings. I do not want to hurt your feelings. Just forgive a fellow who is too dumb to know better. I may not be a good Christian, but I am still a Christian. I am a member of the body of Christ. I am in the ark along with the blessed few who have been honored by God with grace, and for that reason I am not ashamed and I do not want you to be.

We want a separated-from-the-world, heads-up, knees-bent, living church! Sure we can have our skating parties, gatherings, and coffees. Nothing is wrong with that, provided we know that we do not need it. These activities are something on the side so we can relax. Jesus Christ is our center, and so the way to get in is by faith and confession.

6

A MODEL CHURCH

Church people imitate models, and Christians have had a habit of going off on tangents, following moods, modes, and habits. We wish it were different, but down the years we have been like a flock of sheep, everybody following everybody else. We have models and we follow them. The church tends to decline in moral power if it chooses the wrong model or an inadequate model. Now don't interrupt me by saying, "Jesus is our model." I know that He is our model—He ought to be our model. But the simple fact is that He is not. He ought to be the model for the churches, but Jesus Christ has about as much authority in the average Protestant church as I have in the average Catholic church.

I heard about a scientist, Jean Henri Fabre, studying one of the species of caterpillars. He got a huge round vessel, a large crock, and put a lot of caterpillars called army worms around the outside bumper-to-bumper. Then he started them moving. Actually he didn't have to start them—they are called army worms because they are always marching. As far as Fabre could tell, no caterpillar knew where it was going: it was following the tail of the one ahead of it, and the one that was after it followed its tail. Each followed the one ahead until they got clear around to the original one that was following the tail of the one ahead of it. Around and around the crock they went. In nature, army worms march across and through the woods and forest and bushes in a straight line. But because they had been tricked and put on a circular path, they went around and around until one after another they fell off.

In the United States I can take you to beautiful little churches with the doors nailed up—all of those blessed religious army worms that once went around in a circle fell off and were buried in the backyard. Now there is nobody there; they have all fallen off. They ran around, chased each other, and took each other for models. Now it is all over and there is nothing left but gravestones, green briers, bats, and memories.

The Thessalonican church had taken the right models. Their models were God and Paul the apostle. Because they had taken the right models, other people took them for a model. Paul was proud and happy that other people—including the Macedonians and Achaians—were talking about the Christians at Thessalonica. He said, "Your faith to God-ward is spread abroad; so that we need not to speak any thing. For they themselves shew of us what manner of entering in we had unto you, and how ye turned to God from idols to serve the living and true God" (1 Thessalonians 1:8–9).

The church at Thessalonica was a model church, and I want it to be the pattern for our church. We are to be a model church, a church that people, when they hear about it, will say is a Christian church if ever one was.

If people will follow other people, then they ought to follow the right kind of people in the right direction. If religious people will parade, then we ought to get them parading in the right way. To a large extent evangelicals have been given wrong models. While we talk about the Lord Jesus and fight for the creeds that say He is the Lord of Glory, He has very little to say among us. Who even pretends to obey the Sermon on the Mount? Some dispensationalists have even ruled it out, so it is not even theologically necessary to believe it anymore. It belongs to some other dispensation. That kind of rules out the whole business. Who even pretends to obey the First Corinthians epistle dealing with marriage, litigation, and the Lord's Supper?

FEATURES OF A MODEL CHURCH

The model church must embody certain features. An important one is following the order of the New Testament by letting Scripture decide matters.

I knew a man from India who got hold of a New Testament, was converted, and started to preach, but he had no background at all. That is, he started from scratch. He did not have a Greek Orthodox or Roman Catholic or Protestant background. He just started from the beginning. He didn't know anything about churches. He testified, "What I did when I had a problem in the church was to go straight to the New Testament and settle it. I let the New Testament tell me what I was to do." The result was that God greatly blessed him and his work in the land of India.

This is what I would like to see in our church—the New Testament order of letting Scripture decide matters. When it comes to a question—any question—what does the Word of God say? All beliefs and practices should be tested by the Word; no copying unscriptural church methods.

WE SHOULD LET
THE WORD OF GOD DECIDE

I would also have in our body the power of the Spirit of Christ. I have said that the average gospel church could get along without the Holy Spirit—and many do. We are praying for revival. What is revival? It is when the Holy Spirit takes over the work that is His, instead of being pushed aside into the benediction. He now becomes the Chief Executive of the church, running it. "But ye shall receive power, after that the Holy Ghost is come upon you" (Acts 1:8). That means that the Spirit of heaven should come to a company on earth with His all-prevailing gifts, power, and grace, with His life, His illumination, and His discernment. This is not fanaticism; this is not any weird religion. This is just what the Bible teaches.

As a church we must also embody in a supreme degree the purposes for which we exist. There are three purposes for which we exist on earth: to worship, to witness, and to work. When people are converted they immediately change their citizenships. They are no longer citizens of earth except in a provisory way. They are now citizens of heaven.

Abraham, when he went down from Ur of the Chaldees, was called a Hebrew, a man from the other side of the river, a stranger. He spoke with an accent. He brought different habits: eating habits, dressing habits, speech habits, and other customs. He brought them from Ur of the Chaldees. He was a different man, a stranger and a foreigner there.

WE IMMEDIATELY SWITCH CITIZENSHIP

Christians, when they are born of God, immediately shift their citizenships and become pilgrims and strangers where they used to be citizens. "I am a stranger here/upon a foreign land/ my home is far away/beyond the golden strand," we used to sing. Why then does God leave us here? Why are we here at all? All who are born anew have new natures. God becomes our Father and Jesus becomes our Brother, we become the habitation of the Spirit and heaven is our fatherland. Why then are we left here on earth among strangers? We are left here to worship, to witness, and to work. Those three things are what we are here for.

WE ARE HERE TO WORSHIP

Our worship must be in the Spirit. Jesus said, "God is a Spirit: and they that worship him must worship him in spirit and in truth" (John 4:24). To worship in such a way that God will accept it, there must be individual committal to Christ and inward purification by blood and fire. There must be separation from the world, from its opinions, habits, and values. But right now we are just coming out of a period when people were so eager to make converts that they fell into a trap that Jesus Christ warned them about. He said, "For ye compass sea and land to make one proselyte, and when he is made, ye make him twofold more the child of hell than yourselves" (Matthew 23:15).

We are just coming through that period when John 3:16 was the only verse anybody used. The Lord loves everybody. Come, come, come; everybody get converted. So people came, but their conversions were backward. In place of the people being converted into the kingdom of God, the church was converted over to their habits and ways. There was no separation from the world; the world's opinions and habits came into the church.

Do you want God to bless you? You say, "We want God to bless us. We believe the Lord is coming." Did you read the Bible or watch TV more this week? Think of the time you have spent. How many half-hour periods did you spend with your Bible, and how many did you spend with amusements? We do not take our faith seriously enough.

WE ARE HERE TO WITNESS

We are here to worship; we are here to get rid of the habits and values of the world; and we are here to witness. What is a witness? A witness is somebody who testifies to a personal experience. Have you ever thought of the unscriptural, hopeless situation we are in now in evangelical churches? The preacher is the only soul-winner. If he does not come through and win souls, the church declines. The Lord never meant it to be so. He meant that everybody should be a witness.

What should we be witnesses to? We are witnesses only to our personal experiences. Go into a court of law and say, "Well, Aunt Mabel told me . . ." and they will shut you up immediately. We do not care what Aunt Mabel said. What do *you* know? What did you see? What did you feel? What did you hear? What did you taste? What came within the confines of your personal experience? The Lord says, "Ye shall be witnesses unto me" (Acts 1:8). Go tell everybody.

But suppose somebody says, "How do you know?" Then we can smile and say, "I was there—I know." I was converted, and I know I was converted. I was present, so I know. Nobody can argue me out of it.

When I was young, I used to read books dealing with atheism. I tried to acquaint myself as best I could with everything that was against Christianity. I deliberately bought and read books aimed to prove that Christianity was not true, that the Bible was a hoax, that Jesus Christ was a myth, and that the whole thing was subjective self-deception. When I had read the books, I could not answer them. I did not know how to answer them, but I knew one thing. "Hold on a minute," I would say to the authors. "I happen to know. I was there. You are trying to argue me down by reasoning, but I can tell you by experience that I know." More than one time, I got on my knees and with tears near the surface worshiped Jesus Christ, God's Son. I did not know the answers to their arguments, but I knew the One against whom they were arguing. A witness is somebody who has been there and who knows by experience.

WE ARE HERE TO WORK

The third reason we are in the world is to do good works. They call that benevolence in the churches. A fellow drives up in an expensive car, his wife gets out wearing a genuine fur coat, he parks and finally wanders in wearing a fine wool suit. The church members pass around a plate for benevolence and he puts in a dime. We owe the world good works. God anointed Jesus Christ with the Holy Spirit and power, and Jesus went about doing good and healing all who were oppressed by the devil. Jesus did good works and said, "As my Father hath sent me, even so send I you" (John 20:21). You and I are in the world not to put a thin, apologetic dime in the basket, but we are here to share with others around the world.

I pray to God Almighty that I may not live my life out and when I am gone not have anybody sorry I went. It is entirely possible. Doing good works is not just benevolence, either. It is doing good works for Jesus Christ's sake. That is why you are left here. Otherwise you would be in heaven, sitting around tuning your harp. Instead you are down here doing good works.

How do I do good works? I do them by prayer and by my money. There is a beautiful passage where Jesus tells a parable and then explains it. He says, "Make to yourselves friends of the mammon of unrighteousness; that, when ye fail, they may receive you into everlasting habitations" (Luke 16:9). The stingiest old miser that ever lived only needs two pennies when he is dead—one for each eye. In other words, by the right and generous use of my money I can bless people whom I have never seen. When the end comes and money does not help me anymore, there will be people there and God will say to them, "This is the man who kept you two years when you were a displaced child over there. His money helped you." They never knew who it was. Good works are beautiful, and churches ought to be doing them.

Is it fanaticism that a church ought to worship, to witness, and to work? I do not think so. If we do those three things rightly we will have very little time left for anything else.

Suppose someone asks, "What do you do?" There are all sorts of things you can do. You can pray and you can watch for God's providential openings. You can do good works and follow Jesus who was anointed with the Holy Spirit to do good works.

MUST BE A CHANGE IN WAY OF LIFE

Here is what grieves me, and I believe this also grieves the Holy Spirit: my hearers rise to this call emotionally, but they will not confirm it by a corresponding change in their way of life. Their goodness is like the morning clouds—by nine o'clock the sun has burnt off the fog. This is what happens to many people's good intentions. They rise emotionally to an urgent message that we become a New Testament church, that we become a model church, that we have the order of the New Testament and the power of the Holy Spirit in order that we might worship, work, and witness. Emotionally they rise to it, but they will not confirm their emotions by corresponding changes in their way of life.

They want to be blessed by God, but they want God to bless them on their terms. They look pensively to God for victory, but they will not bring their giving into line. They will not practice family prayer, rushing off without it. They will not take time for secret prayer and will not forgive those who have wronged them. They will not seek to be reconciled to those with whom they have quarreled. They will not pick up their crosses and say,

"Jesus, I my cross have taken, all to leave and follow Thee."

What is going to bring about the model church? Do you think that it ever can come within a church?

Is there too much dead wood? Are there too many wrong directions, or too many things wrong with us? Are we like an old person who has every organ in the body gone bad? The doctor looks the person over and says, "There is nothing I can do for you. Go home and wait." Are we like that? Or is there hope?

I believe there is hope. It is going to cost a little bit. In fact, it is going to cost quite a bit. "If any man will come after me, let him deny himself, and take up his cross, and follow me" (Matthew 16:24). It is never fun carrying a cross. Isn't it strange that Jesus made a bloody, pain-filled cross a symbol of His religion?

Modern churches have made fun a symbol of their religion. I want to grieve, bury my head in my hands, and sob before God when I hear, as I often do, precious young people, whom I would give my blood for, get up and in a little, tiny voice say, "Oh, I am so glad I have found out that you do not have to be a sinner to have fun. We have fun in the church, too. You can follow Jesus and have fun." Then they sit down. How they have been betrayed! It is the cross that is the symbol of the Christian life. But we will not pick up our cross. We will not forgive our enemies. We will not be reconciled.

A RAKING OF
CARNAL, DEAD LEAVES

The average church is simply a raking together of carnal, dead leaves, without any life. We organize it, give to support it, and keep it up. Still we have nothing but carnal leaves that will burn in hell in the days before us when our Lord returns.

I believe there is hope, and I believe there is a lot of it. It is going to take a bit of grit and determination and a good deal of prayer and cross-bearing. But we will have God on our side, and I would rather have God on my side than all the armies of the world. He will confirm the word of His servant; He will perform the counsel of His messenger. "I will make darkness light before them, and crooked things straight. These things will I do unto them, and not forsake them" (Isaiah 42:16).

He will give fruit if we will but trust Him and dare to believe. Have you got the Christian courage to change your home to suit the will of God? Have you got the Christian courage to bring your business into line with the will of God? Have you got the Christian courage to bring your personal life into line with the will of God, to purge everything that is not of God? We have yet to know how desperately we need God to do something in this terrible day in which we live, a day of worldliness, carnality, competition, and vainglory. How we need God; how we need Christ; how we need the Holy Spirit. We need clean living, sanctification, and purity of heart. Then the Spirit of the Living God will come upon us.

Some say, "This is a gloomy business you are preaching." When the Moravians went through this, they were anointed of God. Historians said of them that they went out from the church not knowing whether they were still on earth or had already died and gone to heaven. The joy of the Lord was radiantly beautiful upon them, and they became happy people.

"John Wesley," Dr. Johnson said, "was the greatest example

of sheer moral happiness that I ever knew." I am not preaching a gloomy religion to you. I am only telling you there must be a new direction set. We must seek the Lord. One glimpse of His face will take away all our carnal desires for anything less than that.

Then the hungry-hearted, the thirsty, the disillusioned, the disappointed, and the sick will come our way. They will come because they will want to come, and they will know why they are coming. They will not come because a person invited them but because of Christ Jesus. The church will begin to grow. It will grow in power, in grace, in numbers, in usefulness, in prestige, and in influence. Everybody will know it is the church that the Lord has blessed.

As written in Isaiah 60, God said about Jerusalem, in effect, "I am going to bless you. I am going to put a crown on you and I am going to send my blessings over you like doves to their nest. Everybody that passes by will point and say, 'That is the city which the Lord has blessed.'" That is what I want to see in our church. We should become the kind of church that the Lord has blessed. This is the reformation necessary within Protestantism.

God has His seed of survival. He has His people who are ready to say, "God, we want to have biblical order, and we want to have the power of the Holy Spirit. We want to fulfill Your will in worship, witness, and work. We are willing to back up our desires by carrying the cross and by bringing our lives into line with Your desires."

INTEGRATION
OR REPUDIATION?

The world seems to possess a real genius for being wrong, even the educated world. We might just let that pass and go fishing except that we Christians happen to be living in the world and we have an obligation to be right—in everything, all of the time. We cannot afford to be wrong.

I can see how a right man might live in a wrong world and not be much affected by it except that the world will not let him alone. It wants to educate him. It is forever coming up with some new idea, which, by the way, is usually an old idea dusted off and shined up for the occasion, and demanding that everyone, including the said right man, conform on pain of deep-seated frustration or a horrible complex of some kind.

Society, being fluid, usually moves like the wind, going all out in one direction until the novelty wears off or there is a war or a depression. Then the breeze sets another way and everyone is supposed to go along with it without asking too many questions, though this constant change of direction should certainly cause the thoughtful soul to wonder whether anyone really knows what all the excitement is about after all.

Right now the zephyrs are blowing in the direction of social integration, sometimes also called social adjustment. According to this notion society is possessed of a norm, a sort of best-of-all-possible model after which we must all pattern ourselves if we want to escape sundry psychosomatic disorders and emotional upsets. The only safety for any of us is in becoming so well adjusted to the other members of society as to reduce the nervous and mental friction to a minimum. Education therefore should first of all teach adjustment to society. Whatever people happen to be interested in at the moment must be accepted as normal, and any nonconformity on the part of anyone is bad for the individual and harmful to everybody. Our highest ambition should be to become integrated to the mass, to lose our moral individuality in the whole.

However absurd this may appear when thus stated baldly, it is nevertheless a fair description of the most popular brand of philosophy now engaging the attention of society. So many and so efficient are the media of mass communication that when the Brahmans of the educational world decide that it is time for the wind to change, the commonalty quickly get the drift and swing obediently into the breeze. Anyone who resists is a killjoy and a spoilsport, to say nothing of being old-fashioned and dogmatic.

Well, if to escape the charge of being dogmatic I must accept the changing dogmas of the masses, then I am willing to be known as a dogmatist and no holds barred. We who call ourselves Christians are supposed to be a people apart. We claim to have repudiated the wisdom of this world and adopted the wisdom of the cross as the guide of our lives. We have thrown in our lot with that One who while He lived on earth was the most unadjusted of the sons of men. He would not be integrated into society. He stood above it and condemned it by withdrawing from it even while dying for it. Die for it He would, but surrender to it He would not.

The wisdom of the cross is repudiation of the world's "norm." Christ, not society, becomes the pattern of the Christian life. The believer seeks adjustment, not to the world, but to the will of God, and just to the degree that he is integrated into the heart of Christ is he out of adjustment with fallen human society. The Christian sees the world as a sinking ship from which he escapes not by integration but by abandonment.

A new moral power will flow back into the Church when we stop preaching social adjustment and begin to preach social repudiation and cross carrying. Modern Christians hope to save the world by being like it, but it will never work. The Church's power over the world springs out of her unlikeness to it, never from her integration into it.

8

SURE! PAY THAT INCOME TAX

A reader of *The Alliance Weekly* writes to inquire about the federal income tax. Her question is right to the point, "Should we pay it or not?"

It had never occurred to me that there could be any doubt in anyone's mind about the Christian's obligation toward the income tax, but if one person is troubled about it maybe there are others, so here are a few thoughts, as the political orators say, "along that line."

Spies, feigning themselves just men, once came to Jesus with the question, "Is it lawful to give tribute unto Caesar, or not?" (Matthew 22:17). These spies were obviously using an honest question to entrap our Lord. The problem they brought to the Savior was one that had been bothering a lot of good people and if it had been asked in sincerity would have been altogether right and proper. Our Lord with His amazing penetration answered the question for all men of goodwill—and did it without falling into the trap so carefully set for Him.

His answer has become celebrated. "Render therefore unto Caesar the things which are Caesar's; and unto God the things that are God's" (Matthew 22:21). Neither the Romans nor the Jewish authorities could object to this injunction, since no one would dare to admit he wanted anything that was not his.

Any way the word stands, render to governmental authorities whatever by legal right belongs to them. And since they determine what is legally theirs, it is the duty of the Christian to pay—withholding only that over which earthly powers have no right, viz., worship, supreme love, and the moral and spiritual claims of the Most High God. These are the things that belong to God alone; and where earthly governments infringe upon them it is and always will be the sacred obligation of every Christian to resist to the death.

Since it is usually not good practice to rest an entire case upon one passage of Scripture, look also at Paul's words to the Roman Christians:

> Let every soul be subject unto the higher powers. For there is no power but of God: the powers that be are ordained of God. Whosoever therefore resisteth the power, resisteth the ordinance of God: and they that resist shall receive to themselves damnation. . . . Wherefore ye must needs be subject, not only for wrath, but also for conscience sake. For for this cause pay ye tribute also: for they are God's ministers, attending continually upon this very thing. Render therefore to all their dues: tribute to whom tribute is due; custom

to whom custom; fear to whom fear; honour to whom honour. (Romans 13:1–2, 5–7)

When we remember that "tribute" is *taxes* and is so rendered in many translations, the question of whether or not a Christian should pay his income tax seems no longer to be in doubt. The answer of Christ and Paul is, Yes.

While human governments ("the powers that be") are ordained of God, it does not follow that the rulers or officials of a given country are therefore always just and wise. They can and do err in their judgments and often impose ordinances that are anything but judicious and levy taxes unreasonably high.

It is my opinion that our present federal income tax will prove in the long run to work against the interests of the country. It is altogether possible for a nation to tax itself out of existence. Taxes are absolutely necessary as being the only source of revenue for the maintenance of the government, but when things get so out of hand that it is legally possible for the tax collector (that he has recently become a "director" doesn't make him any the less odious) to take away from a citizen as much as 90 percent of his income, surely history is waving a red lantern in front of us. Unless we slow down, we may crash financially and go the way of those nations and empires of yesterday that have left only their crumbling ruins to bear testimony to their departed glory.

What then shall we do? As Christians, pay our taxes exactly as commanded us in the Word of God. As citizens of a democratic country, do whatever we in conscience believe will improve the quality of our leadership and postpone as long as possible the inevitable disaster. And above all things, let "supplications, prayers, intercessions, and giving of thanks, be made for all men; For kings, and for all that are in authority; that we may lead a quiet and peaceable life in all godliness and honesty" (1 Timothy 2:1–2).

9

MEASURING SPIRITUALITY BY PUBLIC PRAYERS

The depths of a man's spirituality may be known quite accurately by the quality of his public prayers.

Bible prayers remain the most perfect examples of what prayer should be to please most our heavenly Father. How bold they are, yet how respectful; how intimate, yet how deeply reverent.

Those who heard Luther's prayers have told us of the tremendous effect they often had upon the listeners. He would begin in moving humility, his spirit facedown in utter self-abnegation, and sometimes rise to a boldness of petition that would startle the hearers.

There is among us today a pseudo-mysticism that affects a tender intimacy with God but lacks that breathless awe which the true worshiper must always feel in the presence of the Holy God. This simpering spirit sometimes expresses itself in religious baby talk wholly unworthy of those who are addressing the Most High.

To hear a so-called Christian cooing in a voice indelicately familiar, addressing words of saccharine sweetness to one whom he or she calls "Jesus dear," is a shocking experience for anyone who has once seen heaven opened and stood speechless before the Holy Presence. No one who has ever bowed before the burning bush can thereafter speak lightly of God, much less be guilty of levity in addressing Him.

When Horace Bushnell prayed in the field under the night sky, his friend who knelt by his side drew in his arms close to his body. "I was afraid to stretch out my hands," he said, "lest I touch God."

While prayers are not addressed to the listeners, they are, nevertheless, meant to be heard by them and should be made with that knowledge frankly in mind. Paul makes this perfectly clear in his first Corinthian epistle. Finney had much to say about this also, as did certain others of the religious great.

We would do well in these days of superficialities in religion to rethink the whole matter of public prayer. It will lose nothing of spiritual content from being subjected to prayerful thought and reverent criticism.

10

WANTED: COURAGE WITH MODERATION

S in has done a pretty complete job of ruining us, and the process of restoration is long and slow. The works of grace in the individual life may be never so clear and definite, but it is indeed the labor of God to bring the once fallen heart back into the divine likeness again. In nothing is this seen more plainly than in the great difficulty we experience in achieving spiritual symmetry in our lives. The inability of even the most devout souls to show forth the Christian virtues in equal proportion and without admixture of un-Christlike qualities has been the source of heartache to how many of God's believing people.

The virtues before us, courage and moderation, when held in correct proportion, make for a well-balanced life and one of great usefulness in the kingdom of God. Where one is missing or present only in minute degree, the result is a life out of balance and powers wasted.

Almost any sincere writing, if examined closely, will be found to be autobiographic. We know best what we have ourselves experienced. This article is not an exception. I may as well admit frankly that it is autobiographic, for the discerning reader will discover the truth no matter how hard I may try to conceal it.

Briefly, I have seldom been called a coward, even by my most cordial enemies, but my want of moderation has sometimes caused grief to my dearest friends. An extreme disposition is not easy to tame, and the temptation to bring severe, immoderate methods to the aid of the Lord is one not easily resisted. The temptation is further strengthened by the knowledge that it is next to impossible to pin a preacher down and make him eat his words. There is a ministerial immunity accorded a man of God, which may lead Boanerges into extravagant and irresponsible language unless he uses heroic measures to bring his nature under the sway of the Spirit of love. This I have sometimes failed to do, and always to my own real sorrow.

Here again the contrast between the ways of God and the ways of man is seen. Apart from such wisdom as painful experience may give, we are prone to try to secure our ends by direct attack, to rush the field and win by assault. That was Samson's way, and it worked well except for one minor oversight: it slew the victor along with the vanquished! There is a wisdom in the flank attack, but a wisdom that the rash spirit is likely to reject.

Of Christ it was said, "He shall not cry, nor lift up, nor cause his voice to be heard in the street. A bruised reed shall he not break, and the smoking flax shall he not quench: he shall bring forth judgment unto truth" (Isaiah 42:2–3). He achieved His tremendous purposes without undue physical exertion and altogether without violence. His whole life was marked by moderation; yet He was of all men the most utterly courageous. He could send back word to Herod who had threatened Him, "Go ye, and tell that fox, Behold, I cast out devils, and I do cures to day and to morrow, and the third day I shall be perfected" (Luke 13:32). There is consummate courage here, but no defiance, no sign of contempt, no extravagance of word or act. He had courage with moderation.

The failure to achieve balance between these virtues has caused much evil in the church through the years, and the injury is all the greater when church leaders are involved. Lack of courage is a grave fault and may be a real sin when it leads to compromise in doctrine or practice. To sit back for the sake of peace and allow the enemy to carry off the sacred vessels from the temple is never the part of a true man of God. Moderation to the point of surrender where holy things are concerned is certainly not a virtue; but pugnacity never yet won when the battle was a heavenly one. The fury of man never furthered the glory of God. There is a right way to do things, and it is never the violent way. The Greeks had a famous saying: "Moderation is best": and the homely proverb of the American farmer, "Easy does it," has in it a wealth of profound philosophy.

God has used, and undoubtedly will yet use, men in spite of their failure to hold these qualities in proper balance. Elijah was a man of courage; no one could doubt that, but neither would anyone be so rash as to claim that he was a man of patience or moderation. He carried the day by assault, by challenge, and was not above satire and abuse when he thought it would help things; but when the enemy was confounded, he went into a tailspin and sank into the depths of despair. That is the way of the extreme nature, of the man of courage without moderation.

Eli, on the other hand, was a man of moderation. He could not say "no" even to his own family. He loved a weak peace, and stark tragedy was the price he paid for his cowardice. Both these men were good men, but they could not find the happy mean. Of the two, fiery Elijah was certainly the greater man. It is painful to think what Eli would have done in Elijah's circumstances. And I could pity even Hophni and Phinehas if Elijah had been their father!

This leads us logically to think of Paul, the apostle. Here is a man whom we need never take at a discount. He seems to have had an almost perfect courage along with a patient disposition and a forbearance truly Godlike. What he might have been apart from grace is seen in the brief description given of him before his conversion. After he had helped to stone Stephen to death, he went out Christian hunting, "yet breathing out threatenings" (Acts 9:1). Even after his conversion he was capable of summary judgments when he felt strongly on a question. His curt rejection of Mark after he had gone back from the work was an example of his short way of dealing with men in whom he had lost confidence. But time and suffering and an increasing intimacy with the patient Savior seems to have cured this fault in the man of God. His later days were sweet with love and fragrant with forbearance and charity. So should it be with all of us.

It is a significant thing that the Bible gives no record of a coward ever being cured of his malady. No "timid soul" ever grew into a man of courage. Peter is sometimes cited as an exception, but there is nothing in his record that would mark him as a timid man either before or after Pentecost. He did touch the borderline once or twice, it is true, but for the most part he was a man of such explosive courage that he was forever in trouble for his boldness.

How desperately the church at this moment needs men of courage is too well known to need repetition. Fear broods over the church like some ancient curse. Fear for our living, fear of our jobs, fear of losing popularity, fear of each other: these are the ghosts that haunt the men who stand today in places of church leadership. Many of them, however, win a reputation for courage by repeating safe and expected things with comical daring. Yet self-conscious courage is not the cure. To cultivate the habit of "calling a spade a spade" may merely result in our making a nuisance of ourselves and doing a lot of damage in the process. The ideal seems to be a quiet courage that is not aware of its own presence. It draws its strength each moment from the indwelling Spirit and is hardly aware of *self* at all. Such a courage will be patient also and well balanced and safe from extremes. May God send a baptism of such courage upon us.

11

THE HONEST USE OF RELIGIOUS WORDS

A disturbing phenomenon of the day is the new and tricky use of familiar words.

A "people's republic," for instance, is not a republic nor does it belong to the people. The word "freedom" now in most countries refers to something so restricted that a generation or two ago another word altogether would have been chosen to describe it.

Other words that have changed their meanings without admitting it are "war," "peace," "grant" (to describe the small sop the government tosses back out of the money it has previously taken from us), "right," "left," "equality," "security," "liberal," and many more. These have been emptied of their meaning, and a different meaning has been poured into them. We may now read them or hear them spoken and, unless we are very sharp, gain from them a wholly false idea.

This phenomenon has invaded the field of religion also. In a predominantly Christian society such as prevails in the West the words of Scripture and of Christian theology have quite naturally acquired a fixed meaning and until recently always meant the same thing whenever they were used by educated and responsible persons. With the coming of the various revolutions—scientific, industrial, philosophical, social, artistic, political—fixed meanings have deserted religious words and now float about like disembodied spirits, looking for but apparently never finding the bodies from which they have been exorcised by the revolutionists.

Among religious words that have lost their Christian meaning are "inspiration," "revelation," "spiritual," "fellowship," "brotherhood," "unity," "worship," "prayer," "heaven," "immortality," "hell," "Lord," "new birth," "converted"—but the list is long and includes almost every major word of the Christian faith.

Of course I do not refer here to the translation of a word from one language to another, nor to the slow evolution that takes place in the forms of words over the years. I refer to the deliberate use of old and familiar words with fixed meanings in a way that violates those meanings and makes the words convey ideas other than those the hearer has every right to expect. The speaker may employ an orthodox word but he does not mean what the hearer thinks he means, so the hearer is deceived. This is a dishonest use of words.

This trick is reprehensible anywhere, but when used deliberately in the sphere of religion it is no less than an act of sheer moral turpitude.

The constant use of biblical terms to express nonbiblical concepts is now common. Yet not everyone who misuses religious words is guilty of wrong intent. For two full generations the habit of emptying words of one meaning and refilling them with another has been taking place among the churches; so it is quite natural that many sincere ministers should engage in theological double talk without knowing it.

Certain biblical words along with certain theological terms embody what God has given to be intellectually grasped by man. It is critically important that the same word should mean the same thing to everyone in a given language group. To permit a change in meaning is to invite disaster. To preserve life the physician and the druggist use words of fixed meaning common to both. How much more should the pulpit and the pew have a clear understanding about the words of eternal life.

The modern effort to popularize the Christian faith has been extremely damaging to that faith. The purpose has been to simplify truth for the masses by using the language of the masses instead of the language of the church. It has not succeeded, but has added to rather than diminished religious confusion.

Positive beliefs are not popular these days. A mistaken desire to maintain a spirit of tolerance among all races and religions has produced a breed of Januslike Christians with built-in swivels, remarkable only for their ability to turn in any direction gracefully. The philosophy behind this whole thing is that religious beliefs are matters of personal choice, and that the Lord adapts His saving truth to the individual, varying it according to the cultural background, educational level, and social situation of each one. Whatever this is, it is not Christianity.

A number of popular religious books have appeared of late quite literally filled with swivel-words of uncertain meaning; and because these were written by persons ostensibly evangelical, they have been accepted and promoted by the evangelicals. And they are having a real influence on Christian thinking; or more to the point, they are making sound Christian thinking impossible for those who read and admire them. We had better take a good hard look at these books. If the authors will not stand still to let their meanings be examined, there is probably a good reason. Great ideas have a habit of inhabiting the same great words generation after generation. To ignore or reject the word is to reject the idea.

The hope of the church yet lies in the purity of her theology, that is, her beliefs about God and man and their relation to each other. These beliefs have been revealed to her by the inspiration of the Holy Spirit in the sacred Scriptures. Everything there is clear-cut and accurate. We dare not be less than accurate in our treatment of anything so precious.

12

THE RIGHT ATTITUDE TOWARD OUR SPIRITUAL LEADERS

We have and will always have spiritual leaders.

Even the most democratic-minded Christian is being influenced, and so led to some degree, by some other Christian living or dead. He cannot escape it; that is the way he is made and he might as well accept it.

At the extreme ends of the religious spectrum are those churches that are controlled from the top by an all-powerful hierarchy and those churches that boldly reject any such supreme authority and insist upon complete autonomy within the local assembly. Yet both kinds of churches are controlled by their leaders. The one group admits it, the other denies it; but the control exists for both nevertheless. Admittedly the degree of control is less in the second instance than in the first, but it is there.

That our religious outlook is largely determined for us by our leaders cannot be denied, but whether that is a good or an evil will depend altogether upon the kind of leaders we have and the wisdom we exercise in our attitude toward them.

I think we make two mistakes in our attitude toward our Christian leaders, one in not being sufficiently grateful to them and the other in following them too slavishly.

The first is a sin of omission, and because it is something that is not there it is not so likely to be noticed as a sin that is plainly present. For instance, it is a sin to be ungrateful to a man who has befriended us, but it is not as bad or as obvious a sin as stealing his pocketbook.

To be grateful to God's servants is to be grateful to God. The benefits we receive from them result from God's working through them, but as free agents they could have refused to cooperate. That they cheerfully yielded their members to the Spirit for our good puts us under continual obligation to them. Because they are so many, and because the vast majority of them have long fallen asleep, we cannot make a like return to them in person; the only way we can discharge our obligation is to be thankful. Gratitude is an offering precious in the sight of God, and it is one that the poorest of us can make and be not poorer but richer for having made it.

In a very real sense we thank God when we thank His people. Gratitude felt and expressed becomes a healing, life-building force in the soul. Something wonderful happens within us when gratitude enters. We cannot be too grateful, for it would be like loving too much or being too kind. And if we are to make a mistake it had better be on the side of humble gratitude for benefits received. Should we in error give credit to someone who does not deserve it we are far better off than if we fail to give credit to one who does.

To those holy men who gave us the sacred Scriptures we owe a debt we can never hope to pay. We should be glad they were in such a spiritual state that they could hear the Voice at the critical moment when God would use them to transmit His mighty words to mankind. And to all who in olden times lovingly transcribed the Word, we should be thankful, and to the old saints who at various dangerous times in the past risked their lives to preserve the Holy Scriptures inviolate.

There is a common debt that every Christian owes to his fellow Christians; but there is a heavier debt that he owes to particular Christians: to Bible scholars, to translators, to reformers, missionaries, evangelists, revivalists, hymn writers, composers, pastors, teachers, and praying saints. For these we should keep the incense of our grateful prayers rising day and night to the Father of light who is the source and fountain of all our blessings.

If it is a sin of omission to be ungrateful toward our God-ordained leaders and benefactors, it is as surely a sin to be too dependent upon them. Those men who were honored of God to write down the words of the inspired Scriptures hold a unique position in the providence of God and we except them from what follows. We are completely dependent upon the Scriptures for divine truth and in that sense we must follow the words of the inspired writers without question. But no other man holds such a power over us.

We make a serious mistake when we become so attached to the preaching or writing of a great Christian leader that we accept his teaching without daring to examine it. No man is that important in the kingdom of God. We should follow men only as they follow the Lord, and we should keep an open mind lest we become blind followers of a man whose breath is in his nostrils.

No Christian leader but has his blind spot, his unconscious prejudices, and these will influence his teachings. We will have plenty of our own without weakly accepting those of our teachers.

What then shall we do? Learn from every holy man who exercises a ministry toward us, be grateful to every one of them and thankful for all, and then follow Christ. No free believer should ever sell his freedom to another. No Christian is worthy to be the master of other Christians. Christ alone is worthy to be called Master; there is no other.

"But the anointing which ye have received of him abideth in you, and ye need not that any man teach you: but as the same anointing teacheth you of all things, and is truth, and is no lie, and even as it hath taught you, ye shall abide in him" (1 John 2:27).

13

THE "SPIRITUAL-OR-SECULAR" TIGHTROPE

In chapter 6 of John's gospel, the apostle records one of the two known instances when Jesus miraculously fed a multitude of people. Two disciples and an unnamed boy have roles in the Galilean drama: Philip, a man with a calculator; Andrew, a man with a suggestion; and a boy with a lunch he was willing to share. Look at the episode again:

> When Jesus then lifted up his eyes, and saw a great company come unto him, he saith unto Philip, Whence shall we buy bread, that these may eat? And this he said to prove him: for he himself knew what he would do. Philip answered him, Two hundred pennyworth of bread is not sufficient for them, that every one of them may take a little. One of his disciples, Andrew, Simon Peter's brother, saith unto him, There is a lad here, which hath five barley loaves, and two small fishes: but what are they among so many?

And Jesus said, Make the men sit down. Now there was much grass in the place. So the men sat down, in number about five thousand. And Jesus took the loaves; and when he had given thanks, he distributed to the disciples, and the disciples to them that were set down; and likewise of the fishes as much as they would. (John 6:5–11)

Just prior to this miraculous multiplying of the bread and fish, Jesus "went up into a mountain, and there he sat with his disciples" (6:3). The fact is noteworthy. It seems plain that Jesus withdrew purposely from the great press of people who had been pursuing Him.

There are some things that you and I will never learn when others are present. I believe in church and I love the fellowship of the assembly. There is much we can learn when we come together on Sundays and sit among the saints. But there are certain things that you and I will never learn in the presence of other people.

Unquestionably, part of our failure today is religious activity that is not preceded by aloneness, by inactivity. I mean getting alone with God and waiting in silence and quietness until we are charged with God's Spirit. Then, when we act, our activity really amounts to something because we have been prepared by God for it.

BE SURE IT IS THE RIGHT INACTIVITY!

Those among us who practice inactivity generally do not practice the kind of inactivity recommended in the Bible—the kind of quiet waiting on God that our Lord practiced. Some of what we see today is just plain laziness, and the Lord has nothing good to say about the sluggard. There is not one lonely text in the sixty-six books of the Bible that says anything kind about the sluggard. The inactivity that arises out of sheer laziness has no place in the Bible.

There is also the inactivity that stems from fear. People who are fearful of doing anything at all figure they can narrow the area of their peril by doing nothing. They think if they simply stand still, there will be less danger of getting into trouble. God never sanctions this kind of inactivity, for it springs from an unchristian motive.

Others are inactive because they lack vision. They just do not know what to do, so they do nothing! Great sections of the church are in that condition. These are people who have never seen a path, and they do not know where to find one. They have no highway stretching ahead, so they stand still.

But there is an inactivity that, paradoxically, is the highest possible activity. There can be a suspension of the activity of the body, as when our Lord told His disciples to "tarry ye in the city of Jerusalem, until ye be endued with power from on high" (Luke 24:49). They waited. And the Holy Spirit came on them in power.

In the Old Testament, to wait on God meant coming before His presence with expectation and waiting there with physical and mental inactivity. "Cease thy thinking, troubled Christian," one of the old poets wrote. There is a place where the mind quits trying to figure out its own way and throws itself wide open to God. And the shining glory of God comes down into the waiting life and imparts an activity.

Do you understand what I mean when I say that we can go to God with an activity that is inactive? We go to God with a heart that is not acting in the flesh or in the natural—trying to do something. We go to God in an attitude of waiting. It just means that our inner spirit is seeing and hearing and mounting up on wings while our outer, physical person is inactive and even the mind is to some degree suspended.

JESUS ONCE REBUKED A TOO-ACTIVE WOMAN

We know that Jesus once rebuked a woman for being too active. She was Martha of Bethany. Sometimes we are prone to add to what the Lord actually said to Martha. His kindly rebuke has been a cue for preachers to heap abuse upon the poor woman. I personally thank God for the Marthas in the world. Someone generally has to cook and do the dishes and see that the work gets done. Without Marthas, we would not be so sleek and well fed. We should let the Lord's rebuke be sufficient without adding to Martha's chastening.

But notice on the other hand that Mary was there, simply sitting. It is the same word that John uses for the inactivity of Jesus when He went up into the mountain and sat with His disciples. Mary was simply sitting at the feet of the Savior, and the Lord rebuked Martha for her nervous activity. I think she just carried her activity beyond the point where it did any good, and she did not back it up by an inward spiritual relaxation.

Now, in the case of our Lord, the people came to Him, John reports, and He was ready for them. He had been quiet and silent. He had sat alone with His disciples and meditated. Looking upward, He waited until the whole hiatus of divine life moved down from the throne of God into His own soul. He was a violin tuned. He was a battery recharged. He was poised and prepared for the people when they came.

So the people came—a great mob of humanity that three days before had charged out of the surrounding Galilean towns to follow the Teacher. Some brought their babies, and some were elderly and not physically strong for this kind of trekking. Now, after three days on the way, their food had given out. They were in need, but there was no place where they could buy food.

It was then that the Lord asked Philip, "Whence shall we buy bread, that these may eat?" (John 6:5). Does that question say anything to you? It says to me that our human Lord was concerned about bread and people's natural hunger.

I know of no camp meeting ground without a kitchen and dining hall. There has never been a Pentecost that did not have a cook somewhere around the corner to feed the Spirit-filled saints.

Our Lord knows that we are human beings. It is good for us to know that He understands us and our need for food.

OUR BODIES ARE A DISCIPLINE

I have wondered why God gave us bodies and tied us down to them. I have concluded that He did so more or less as a discipline. I do not know what else they are for. Emerson wrote that nature had one function toward human beings, and that was to discipline them.

At least occasionally we are bound to think like this. The body at times gets a little out of hand, and we have to spend as much care and energy looking after it as we spend doing everything else we do. I am glad God understands about it. I am glad He knows. He gave us these mortal frames, and He expects us to take care of them. We see in this setting that He was concerned about the people having something to eat.

I have never believed in the great distinctions that some try to make between the sacred and the secular. Eating can be just as religious an act as praying. It is just as spiritual for me to eat my breakfast as it is to have family prayers. When we separate our breakfast from our prayers, we are making an unnecessary division. Why should we put eating in one category and apologize to the Lord, saying, "I'm awfully sorry, Lord, but You know I have to eat now. I'll see You as soon as I am through, but please excuse me now while I take time to eat."

It is wrong to place our physical necessities on one side and put praying and singing and giving and Bible reading and testifying on the other side. How can we say "This is spiritual" and "This is secular"? We actually try to walk a tightrope between the two, the secular and the spiritual, apologizing to God when we must turn aside for a little while to do something "secular."

Well, I have a better way than that for living, and I can tell you the Lord Jesus never made the distinction that many Christians do. He said He was the Lord. He was God Himself, and He asked, "Where shall we buy bread for these people to eat?" When He broke the loaves and passed them along to that great multitude, they ate, and the eating was as spiritual as the teaching of the preceding days had been. The teaching and the eating were equally spiritual, and the praying that preceded the meal was just as spiritual—but no more so—than the eating.

THE LORD OF OUR BREAD

If you can get hold of that, it will mean a wonderful thing to you. The Lord is the Lord of our bread, the Lord of our eating, the Lord of our bathing, the Lord of our sleeping, the Lord of our dressing, the Lord of our working. When we work we need not say, "I have to work today, but I'll plan to have some time with You this evening." Our Lord is with us, sanctifying everything we do—provided it is honest and good. If your job is decent and respectable, the Lord is going to bless it, and if the Lord is in you, He will be in your labor as well.

Notice that it was the Lord of Glory who said, "Whence shall we buy bread, that these may eat?" (John 6:5). He Himself was concerned with the people's need for food. But He made it Philip's problem. He honored Philip by letting him participate in the solution.

I once preached a sermon in which I said that the Lord is self-sufficient and does not really need us. I bothered some people by that, for they thought the Lord really needed them. They thought that if they should resign or retire, the Lord would have to scramble to find someone who could take their place. What a low view of God! Could you get down on your knees and cry out to a God who needed you? I could not. A God who needed me would be a God in real trouble. God does not have to have me—or you, either. That may be bitter medicine for some to take, because we have come to believe that we are indispensable and that, when we go, a great tree will have fallen, leaving a vacant place against the sky. I am afraid that when some of us die, it will be like a stalk of grass eaten by a grasshopper, and nobody will notice the difference!

But here were these hungry people, and the Lord was going to feed them. The thing is, He did not want just to feed them and have it over with. He wanted some blessing to flow all around as a result of it. So He picked out one of His disciples—Philip— saying to Himself, *I am going to bring Philip into this. I am going to honor him by letting him become a part of this plan. He can help Me work it out, although actually I do not need him at all.*

So Jesus encouraged Philip to tackle the problem along with Him. He nudged Philip a little and got him into a hard spot, just to reveal to Philip his own emptiness.

It is never a waste of time to learn that you do not know every answer, and it is never a waste of time to learn how little you have. It is a positive victory for me when I learn the things I cannot do—and the things that I do not have.

THE LORD CAN
FILL WHAT WE EMPTY

Actually, there is so little filling of our vessels these days because we do so little emptying of them. The Lord had to empty Philip in order that He might fill him, for Philip was full of his own ideas. The Lord cannot fill with His own presence that which is already full of something else. To be frank, Philip did not acquit himself very well when Jesus asked him where they would buy bread for the people to eat.

Philip revealed the type of mind that is altogether earthly, uninspired, and uninspiring. He reached for his calculator, pressed the "on" switch, and went to work. I call him Philip the Calculator.

People are not nicknamed quite as much as they used to be. People used to be nicknamed for what they were. Even in rural western Pennsylvania when I was growing up, people were distinguished by their nicknames. And if you will look back in history, you will find men with distinguishing names, such as Eric the Red and Alexander the Great.

Here in the New Testament was Philip the Calculator— Philip the Mathematician, Philip the Clerk. There was need for a miracle, and Philip set out to calculate the odds. Probably every Christian group has at least one person with a calculator. I have sat on boards for many years, and rarely is there a board without a Philip the Calculator among its members. When you suggest something, out comes the calculator to prove that it cannot be done.

Before our Chicago church relocated, there was an old milk barn on the site. When we talked about building, we had plenty of Philips who said, "It can't be done!" And of course they could prove it. But we built the church anyhow and had the building paid for in six short years. But the Philips said, "It can't be done," and they had the calculations to prove it.

As I say, I have been sitting on these boards for many years, and there are always two kinds of board members: those who can see the miracle and those who can only see their calculators and their strings of calculations. Philip went to work with his calculator. He knew how much money there was among the disciples. He knew how much a loaf of bread cost. He knew the size of the hungry crowd.

ONE HUNDRED
PERCENT NEGATIVE

Philip cranked all those statistics into his calculator and came up with his answer. "Eight months' wages would not buy enough bread for each one to have a bite!" Philip had made his contribution, and it was 100 percent negative. If Jesus and the other disciples had listened only to Philip, they and the multitude would have starved in the wilderness. The glorious miracle would not have taken place.

All you have to do to kill a church is to talk it down. Just let the sheep begin to bleat the blues, and the church will die in no time at all. The power of suggestion will likely care for the rest of the downfall. One fellow will meet another and say, "Things aren't going so well at church, are they?" "No, not so well," the other responds.

Another fellow comes up to man number two: "Things don't seem to be going very well at the church," he comments. "That's what I have been hearing," says man number two. He heard it just five minutes before from man number one. So it soon comes out: "Have you heard what the talk is? Things aren't going very well at the church." Before very long, they have talked that church down. The people with the calculators have seen the problem, but they have not seen God. They have figured things out, but they have not figured God in.

Philip the Calculator. He can be a dangerous man in the church of our Lord Jesus Christ. Every suggestion made in the direction of progress gets a negative vote from this man.

THE MAN
WITH THE SUGGESTION

Next we come to the other man, Andrew. Andrew did a little better than Philip. He made a timid suggestion: "There is a lad here, which hath five barley loaves, and two small fishes: but what are they among so many?" (John 6:9).

I would not call Andrew a world-beater on the basis of this account. If he were living today, he would not be known as a founder or a promoter—that is for sure. Andrew was only partly over on the side of the miracle. Andrew overheard Philip's answer and probably thought, *Surely Philip's final tally is off base. Philip is a good man and I like him, but he is a bit on the negative side.* Andrew looked at all the figures on Philip's printout: so much bread for so many pennies; so many hungry people; break each loaf into so many pieces—*No,* Andrew thought, *it is no use. Philip is right: there would be merely a trifle for each person, even if we had the money. But this can't be the end. There must be an answer. There must be a way.*

So Andrew began to look around. You will be getting a little closer to the miracle when you can get a church full of Andrews. Even if you have only one or two of them, you will usually hear one of them say, "There is a boy here with a lunch, some bread and fish, but then, after all, that's not very much . . ." And there is a rising inflection in his voice, which is an invitation for someone to come to his rescue. "If I can get an encouraging word from someone, I think I can see some hope in this situation." That is Andrew.

You are getting a little warmer when you are like Andrew! Philip was as cold as ice, with his calculator and his proof that no one was going to eat on that occasion. Andrew looked around and said, "Well, we have a start. We have a little lunch here. A little basket. A boy."

I have never been able to figure out how that boy managed to hang onto that lunch. Boys whom I know would have had it eaten by nine o'clock the first morning, and here it was the third day! But he was still holding onto the little lunch. Perhaps his mother had given him some extra food and he still had it. The five loaves were really only pancakes in size and shape. That is all they were—plus two small fish.

So that was the boy. Andrew himself had nothing, but he knew that a boy had a little lunch. The lunch might help out a bit. I think of Andrew as being a help on any church board. At least he was looking around for a fellow with a lunch. This speaks of hopefulness, of at least a little faith.

WE NEED SOME ANDREWS

It is time we find an Andrew or two—people who have hope and faith to look around for at least a token of help. That is all that lunch was: merely a token. It was not very much. It really was not enough for more than one. But Christ took that inadequate token and made it enough for more than five thousand people.

Sometimes I have quoted a little passage I got from dear old Walter Hilton, who lived before the time of Shakespeare. He was talking about serving God and how we ought to go about it. He said, "I will give you a little rule." Then he used the Old English word *mickle*, meaning much. "Mickle have, mickle do. Let have, let do. Nothing have, at least have a good intention." *If you have much, do much. If you haven't much, do what you can. If you haven't anything, have good intentions.* That is a good rule. Andrew at least had good intentions. He found a lunch—a token. He was on God's side.

You may have noticed that John does not really tell us how they got that lunch. He says that Jesus took the loaves; he does not say how He got them. But I have read too much about my Lord to believe that there was any coercion involved. That lunch must have been vitally important to the boy, but he surrendered it to Jesus.

Perhaps Jesus smiled and said to the boy, "Would you like to do something that would help all of these hungry people?" And the happy-faced boy replied, "Certainly, Master."

"Then, may I have your lunch?" I think the boy grinned and handed it over to Jesus, who turned to His disciples and said, "Have the people sit down." So they sat down in orderly rows, in tiers of rows, and Jesus took the bread and blessed it, lifting up His heart and saying, "O God, bless this little bit. Bless this little bit of optimistic hope. Bless this token of belief."

And then Jesus began to spread around the barley bread and the fish, and suddenly there were baskets full. Where did the baskets come from? They were the lunch baskets from which the people had eaten a day or two before. There had been plenty of empty baskets in that crowd, but only one lunch. Jesus took the one lunch and multiplied it so there was food for all. Because it had been surrendered for His use, it became the blessing of more than five thousand people.

SOME PERSONAL QUESTIONS

All of this brings us to some personal questions. Are you a Philip? An Andrew? A boy with a lunch?

Philip was so good at calculations that he forgot to figure God into the equation. Andrew was a little nearer. He did not have anything himself, but he knew where he could dig up something. And then there was the boy. He did not have much, either, but what he had he gave to Jesus, who had the power to make it sufficient.

Which side are you on? Are you with those who are convinced that the Lord cannot do anything in this situation? Do you have out your calculator to prove the situation's impossibility?

Are you among the uncertain ones, whose hearts are on the right side? You are sure that the lunch is not enough, but you are hopeful because it is something.

Perhaps you are with the boy, who says, "If I give You this lunch, Master, it means I may not eat. But I like the way You do things, and I am willing to go along with You. You may take my lunch."

I might as well tell you right here what I think. I think when the Lord sent a basket of that food to the boy, He put an extra fish on top! It would be quite in keeping with the ways of the Lord—to put a little extra in the basket of the fellow who had given his all. I know He does this in spiritual things, so why should He not do it with a lunch?

I recommend that we ask God for at least the faith of an Andrew, and that we begin to look around for tokens of the grace of God. Surely we will find these tokens. You yourself may have a token and not know it. Do you think the boy knew that he had the key to the miracle? No, he did not know. But in fact he carried it in his lunch basket. He had lugged it for three days and did not know it.

You may have in your possession the key to the future. You may have in your hand, without knowing it, the key to the salvation of at least ten people, and perhaps a hundred, if you only knew it. You need only surrender that key to the Lord and let Him have it.

Say to Jesus now, "Master, I only have a token, a little token, but take it, Lord Jesus, take it!" The Lord will take it. How He will multiply it I do not know, but He can do it.

And He will.

THIS WORLD: PLAYGROUND OR BATTLEGROUND?

Things are for us not only what they are; they are what we hold them to be. Which is to say that our attitude toward things is likely in the long run to be more important than the things themselves.

This is a common coin of knowledge, like an old dime, worn smooth by use. Yet it bears upon it the stamp of truth and must not be rejected because it is familiar.

It is strange how a fact may remain fixed, while our interpretation of the fact changes with the generations and the years.

One such fact is the world in which we live. It is here, and has been here through the centuries. It is a stable fact, quite unchanged by the passing of time, but how different is modern man's view of it from the view our fathers held. Here we see plainly how great is the power of interpretation. The world is for all of us not only what it is; it is what we believe it to be. And a tremendous load of woe or weal rides on the soundness of our interpretation.

Going no further back than the times of the founding and early development of our country we are able to see the wide gulf between our modern attitudes and those of our fathers. In the early days, when Christianity exercised a dominant influence over American thinking, men conceived the world to be a battleground. Our fathers believed in sin and the devil and hell as constituting one force; and they believed in God and righteousness and heaven as the other. These were opposed to each other in the nature of them forever in deep, grave, irreconcilable hostility. Man, so our fathers held, had to choose sides; he could not be neutral. For him it must be life or death, heaven or hell, and if he chose to come out on God's side he could expect open war with God's enemies. The fight would be real and deadly and would last as long as life continued here below. Men looked forward to heaven as a return from the wars, a laying down of the sword to enjoy in peace the home prepared for them.

Sermons and songs in those days often had a martial quality about them, or perhaps a trace of homesickness. The Christian soldier thought of home and rest and reunion, and his voice grew plaintive as he sang of battle ended and victory won. But whether he was charging into enemy guns or dreaming of war's end and the Father's welcome home, he never forgot what kind of world he lived in. It was a battleground, and many were the wounded and the slain.

That view of things is unquestionably the scriptural one. Allowing for the figures and metaphors with which the Scriptures abound, it still is a solid Bible doctrine that tremendous spiritual forces are present in the world, and man, because of his spiritual nature, is caught in the middle. The evil powers are bent upon destroying him, while Christ is present to save him through the power of the gospel. To obtain deliverance he must come out on God's side in faith and obedience. That in brief is what our fathers thought; and that, we believe, is what the Bible teaches.

How different today. The fact remains the same but the interpretation has changed completely. Men think of the world, not as a battleground but as a playground. We are not here to fight, we are here to frolic. We are not in a foreign land, we are at home. We are not getting ready to live, we are already living, and the best we can do is to rid ourselves of our inhibitions and our frustrations and live this life to the full. This, we believe, is a fair summary of the religious philosophy of modern man, openly professed by millions and tacitly held by more multiplied millions who live out that philosophy without having given verbal expression to it.

This changed attitude toward the world has had and is having its effect upon Christians, even gospel Christians who profess the faith of the Bible. By a curious juggling of the figures, they manage to add up the column wrong and yet claim to have the right answer. It sounds fantastic but it is true.

That this world is a playground instead of a battleground has now been accepted in practice by the vast majority of evangelical Christians. They might hedge around the question if they were asked bluntly to declare their position, but their conduct gives them away. They are facing both ways, enjoying Christ and the world too, and gleefully telling everyone that accepting Jesus does not require them to give up their fun, and that Christianity is just the jolliest thing imaginable.

The "worship" growing out of such a view of life is as far off center as the view itself, a sort of sanctified nightclubbing without the champagne and the dressed-up drunks.

This whole thing has grown to be so serious of late that it now becomes the bounden duty of every Christian to reexamine his spiritual philosophy in the light of the Bible, and having discovered the scriptural way to follow it, even if to do so he must separate himself from much that he formerly accepted as real but which now in the light of truth he knows to be false.

A right view of God and the world to come requires that we have also a right view of the world in which we live and our relation to it. So much depends upon this that we cannot afford to be careless about it.

15

ARE WE EVANGELICALS SOCIAL CLIMBING?

Traditionally, Christianity has been the religion of the common people. Whenever the upper classes have adopted it in numbers, it has died. Respectability has almost always proved fatal to it.

The reasons back of this are two, one human and the other divine.

Schleiermacher has pointed out that at the bottom of all religion there lies a feeling of dependence, a sense of creature helplessness. The simple man who lives close to the earth lives also close to death and knows that he must look for help beyond himself; he knows that there is but a step between him and catastrophe. As he rises in the social and economic scale, he surrounds himself with more and more protective devices and pushes danger (so he thinks) farther and farther from him. Self-confidence displaces the feeling of dependence he once knew, and God becomes less necessary to him. Should he stop to think this through he would know better than to place his confidence in things and people; but so badly are we injured by our moral fall that we are capable of deceiving ourselves completely and, if conditions favor it, to keep up the deception for a lifetime.

Along with the feeling of security that wealth and position bring comes an arrogant pride that shuts tightly the door of the heart to the waiting Savior. Our Very Important Man may indeed honor a church by joining it, but there is no life in his act. His religion is external and his faith nominal. Conscious respectability has destroyed him.

The second reason Christianity tends to decline as its devotees move up the social scale is that God will not respect persons nor share His glory with another. Paul sets this forth plainly enough in his First Corinthians epistle:

Because the foolishness of God is wiser than men; and the weakness of God is stronger than men. For ye see your calling, brethren, how that not many wise men after the flesh, not many mighty, not many noble, are called: But God hath chosen the foolish things of the world to confound the wise; and God hath chosen the weak things of the world to confound the things which are mighty; And base things of the world, and things which are despised, hath God chosen, yea, and things which are not, to bring to nought things that are: That no flesh should glory in his presence. (1 Corinthians 1:25–29)

When God sent His Son to redeem mankind, He sent Him to the home of a workingman and He grew up to be what we now call a peasant. When He presented Himself to Israel and launched into His earthly ministry, He was rejected by the respectable religionists and had to look for followers almost exclusively from among the poor, plain people. When the Spirit came and the church was founded, its first members were the socially unacceptable. For generations the church drew her numbers from among the lower classes, individual exceptions occurring now and again, of which Saul of Tarsus was the most noteworthy.

During the centuries since Pentecost the path of true Christianity has paralleled pretty closely the path Jesus walked when He was here on earth: it was to be rejected by the great and accepted by the lowly. The institutionalized church has certainly not been poor, nor has she lacked for great and mighty men to swell her membership. But this great church has had no power. Almost always the approval of God has rested upon small and marginal groups whose members were scorned while they lived and managed to gain acceptance only after they had been safely dead several score years.

Today we evangelicals are showing signs that we are becoming too rich and too prominent for our own good. With a curious disregard for the lessons of history we are busy fighting for recognition by the world and acceptance by society. And we are winning both. The great and the mighty are now looking our way. The world seems about to come over and join us. Of course we must make some concessions, but these have almost all been made already except for a bit of compromising here and there on such matters as verbal inspiration, special creation, separation, and religious tolerance.

A. W. TOZER

Evangelical Christianity is fast becoming the religion of the bourgeoisie. The well-to-do, the upper middle classes, the politically prominent, the celebrities are accepting our religion by the thousands and parking their expensive cars outside our church doors, to the uncontrollable glee of our religious leaders who seem completely blind to the fact that the vast majority of these new patrons of the Lord of glory have not altered their moral habits in the slightest nor given any evidence of true conversion that would have been accepted by the saintly fathers who built the churches.

Yes, history is a great teacher, but she cannot teach those who do not want to learn. And apparently we do not.

16

WHY THE WORLD CANNOT RECEIVE

The Spirit of truth; whom the world cannot receive.

JOHN 14:17

The Christian faith, based upon the New Testament, teaches the complete antithesis between the Church and the world. I have noted this briefly in a previous chapter, but the matter is so important to the seeking soul that I feel that I must here go into the whole thing a little further.

It is no more than a religious platitude to say that the trouble with us today is that we have tried to bridge the gulf between two opposites, the world and the Church, and have performed an illicit marriage for which there is no biblical authority. Actually no real union between the world, and the Church is possible. When the Church joins up with the world it is the true Church no longer but only a pitiful hybrid thing, an object of smiling contempt to the world and an abomination to the Lord.

The twilight in which many (or should we say *most?*) believers walk today is not caused by any vagueness on the part of the Bible. Nothing could be clearer than the pronouncements of the Scriptures on the Christian's relation to the world. The confusion that gathers around this matter results from the unwillingness of professing Christians to take the Word of the Lord seriously. Christianity is so entangled with the world that millions never guess how radically they have missed the New Testament pattern. Compromise is everywhere. The world is whitewashed just enough to pass inspection by blind men posing as believers, and those same believers are everlastingly seeking to gain acceptance with the world. By mutual concessions men who call themselves Christians manage to get on with men who have for the things of God nothing but quiet contempt.

This whole thing is spiritual in its essence. A Christian is what he is not by ecclesiastical manipulation but by the new birth. He is a Christian because of a Spirit who dwells in him. Only that which is born of the Spirit is spirit. The flesh can never be converted into spirit, no matter how many church dignitaries work on it. Confirmation, baptism, holy communion, confession of faith—none of these nor all of them together can turn flesh into spirit nor make a son of Adam a son of God. "Because ye are sons," wrote Paul to the Galatians, "God hath sent forth the Spirit of his Son into your hearts, crying, Abba, Father" (Galatians 4:6).

And to the Corinthians he wrote: "Examine yourselves, whether ye be in the faith; prove your own selves. Know ye not your own selves, how that Jesus Christ is in you, except ye be reprobates?" (2 Corinthians 13:5).

And to the Romans: "But ye are not in the flesh, but in the

Spirit, if so be that the Spirit of God dwell in you. Now if any man have not the Spirit of Christ, he is none of his" (Romans 8:9).

That terrible zone of confusion so evident in the whole life of the Christian community could be cleared up in one day if the followers of Christ would begin to follow Christ instead of each other. For our Lord was very plain in His teaching about the believer and the world.

On one occasion, after receiving unsolicited and carnal advice from sincere but unenlightened brethren, our Lord replied: "My time is not yet come: but your time is alway ready. The world cannot hate you; but me it hateth, because I testify of it, that the works thereof are evil" (John 7:6–7).

He identified His fleshly brethren with the world and said that they and He were of two different spirits. The world hated Him but could not hate them because it could not hate itself. A house divided against itself cannot stand. Adam's house must remain loyal to itself or it will tear itself apart. Though the sons of the flesh may quarrel among themselves, they are at bottom one with each other. It is when the Spirit of God comes in that an alien element has entered. The Lord said to His disciples: "If the world hate you, ye know that it hated me before it hated you. If ye were of the world, the world would love his own: but because ye are not of the world, but I have chosen you out of the world, therefore the world hateth you" (John 15:18–19).

Paul explained to the Galatians the difference between the bond child and the free: "But as then he that was born after the flesh persecuted him that was born after the Spirit, even so it is now" (Galatians 4:29).

So throughout the entire New Testament a sharp line is drawn between the Church and the world. There is no middle ground. The Lord recognizes no good-natured "agreeing to disagree" so that the followers of the Lamb may adopt the world's ways and travel along the world's path. The gulf between the true Christian and the world is as great as that which separated the rich man and Lazarus. And furthermore it is the same gulf, that is, it is the gulf that divides the world of ransomed from the world of fallen men.

I well know and feel deeply how offensive such teaching as this must be to the great flock of worldlings that mills around the traditional sheepfold. I cannot hope to escape the charge of bigotry and intolerance that will undoubtedly be brought against me by the confused religionists who seek to make themselves sheep by association. But we may as well face the hard truth that men do not become Christians by associating with church people, nor by religious contact, nor by religious education; they become Christians only by invasion of their nature by the Spirit of God in the new birth. And when they do thus become Christians they are immediately members of a new race, "a chosen generation, a royal priesthood, an holy nation, a peculiar people . . . which in time past were not a people, but are now the people of God: which had not obtained mercy, but now have obtained mercy" (1 Peter 2:9–10).

In the verses quoted there has been no wish to quote out of context nor to focus attention upon one side of truth to draw it away from another. The teaching of these passages is altogether one with all New Testament truth. It is as if we dipped a cup of water from the sea. What we took out would not be all the water in the ocean, but it would be a true sample and would perfectly agree with the rest.

The difficulty we modern Christians face is not misunderstanding the Bible, but persuading our untamed hearts to accept its plain instructions. Our problem is to get the consent of our world-loving minds to make Jesus Lord in fact as well as in word. For it is one thing to say, "Lord, Lord," and quite another thing to obey the Lord's commandments. We may sing, "Crown Him Lord of All," and rejoice in the tones of the loud-sounding organ and the deep melody of harmonious voices, but still we have done nothing until we have left the world and set our faces toward the city of God in hard practical reality. When faith becomes obedience then it is true faith indeed.

The world's spirit is strong, and it clings to us as close as the smell of smoke to our garments. It can change its face to suit any circumstance and so deceive many a simple Christian whose senses are not exercised to discern good and evil. It can play at religion with every appearance of sincerity. It can have fits of conscience (particularly during Lent) and even confess its evil ways in the public press. It will praise religion and fawn on the Church for its ends. It will contribute to charitable causes and promote campaigns to furnish clothing for the poor. *Only let Christ keep His distance and never assert His Lordship over it.* This it will positively not endure. And toward the true Spirit of Christ it will show only antagonism. The world's press (which is always its real mouthpiece) will seldom give a child of God a fair deal. If the facts compel a favorable report, the tone is apt to be condescending and ironic. The note of contempt sounds through.

Both the sons of this world and the sons of God have been baptized into a spirit, but the spirit of the world and the Spirit that dwells in the hearts of twice-born men are as far apart as heaven and hell. Not only are they the complete opposite of each other but they are sharply antagonistic to each other as well. To a son of earth the things of the Spirit are either ridiculous, in which case he is amused, or they are meaningless, in which case he is bored.

But the natural man receiveth not the things of the Spirit of God: for they are foolishness unto him: neither can he know them, because they are spiritually discerned. (1 Corinthians 2:14)

In the first epistle of John two words are used over and over, the words *they* and *ye,* and they designate two wholly different worlds. *They* refers to the men and women of Adam's fallen world; *ye* refers to the chosen ones who have left all to follow Christ. The apostle does not genuflect to the little god Tolerance (the worship of which has become in America a kind of secondary surface religion); he is bluntly intolerant. He knows that tolerance may be merely another name for indifference. It takes a vigorous faith to accept the teaching of the man John. It is so much easier to blur the lines of separation and so offend no one. Pious generalities and the use of *we* to mean both Christians and unbelievers is much safer. The fatherhood of God can be stretched to include everyone from Jack the Ripper to Daniel the Prophet. Thus no one is offended and everyone feels quite snug and ready for heaven. But the man who laid his ear on Jesus' breast was not so easily deceived. He drew a line to divide the race of men into two camps, to separate the saved from the lost, those who shall rise to eternal reward from them that shall sink to final despair. On one side are *they* that know not God;

on the other *ye* (or with a change of person, *we*), and between the two is a moral gulf too wide for any man to cross. Here is the way John states it: "Ye are of God, little children, and have overcome them: because greater is he that is in you, than he that is in the world. They are of the world: therefore speak they of the world, and the world heareth them. We are of God: he that knoweth God heareth us; he that is not of God heareth not us. Hereby know we the spirit of truth, and the spirit of error" (1 John 4:4–6).

Such language as this is too plain to confuse anyone who honestly wants to know the truth. Our problem is not one of understanding, I repeat, but of faith and obedience. The question is not a theological one, What does this teach? It is a moral one, Am I willing to accept this and abide by its consequences? Can I endure the cold stare? Have I the courage to stand up to the slashing attack of the "liberal"? Dare I invite the hate of men who will be affronted by my attitude? Have I independence of mind sufficient to challenge the opinions of popular religion and go along with an apostle? Or briefly, can I bring myself to take up the cross with its blood and its reproach?

The Christian is called to separation from the world, but we must be sure we know what we mean (or more important, what God means) by the *world*. We are likely to make it mean something external only and thus miss its real meaning. The theater, cards, liquor, gambling—these are not the world; they are merely an external manifestation of the world. Our warfare is not against merely an external manifestation of the world. Our warfare is not against mere worldly ways, but against the *spirit* of the world. For man, whether he is saved or lost, is essentially spirit. The world, in the New Testament meaning of the word, is simply unregenerate human nature wherever it is found, whether in a tavern or in a church. Whatever springs out of, is built upon, or receives support from fallen human nature is the world, whether it is morally base or morally respectable.

The ancient Pharisees, in spite of their zealous devotion to religion, were of the very essence of the world. The spiritual principles upon which they built their system were drawn not from above but from below. They employed against Jesus the tactics of men. They bribed men to tell lies in defense of truth. To defend God they acted like devils. To support the Bible they defied the teachings of the Bible. They scuttled religion to save religion. They gave rein to blind hate in the name of the religion of love. There we see the world in all of its grim defiance of God. So fierce was this spirit that it never rested till it had put to death the Son of God Himself. The spirit of the Pharisees was actively and maliciously hostile to the Spirit of Jesus as each was a kind of distillation of the two worlds from whence they came.

Those present-day teachers who place the Sermon on the Mount in some other dispensation than this and so release the Church from its teachings little realize the evil they do. For the Sermon on the Mount gives in brief the characteristics of the kingdom of renewed men. The blessed poor who mourn for their sins and thirst after righteousness are true sons of the kingdom. In meekness they show mercy to their enemies; with guileless candor they gaze upon God; surrounded by persecutors they bless and curse not. In modesty they hide their good deeds. They go out of their way to agree with their adversaries and forgive those who sin against them. They serve God in secret in the depth of their hearts and wait with patience for His open reward. They freely surrender their earthly goods rather than use violence to protect them. They lay up treasures in heaven. They avoid praise and wait for the day of final reckoning to learn who is greatest in the kingdom of heaven.

If this is a fairly accurate view of things, what can we say then when Christian men vie with one another for place and position? What can we answer when we see them hungrily seeking for praise and honor? How can we excuse the passion for publicity, which is so glaringly evident among Christian leaders? What about political ambition in Church circles? What about the fevered palm that is stretched out for more and bigger "love offerings"? What about the shameless egotism among Christians? How can we explain the gross man-worship that habitually blows up one and another popular leader to the size of colossus? What about the obsequious hand-kissing of moneyed men by those purporting to be sound preachers of the gospel?

There is only one answer to these questions; it is simply that in these manifestations we see the world and nothing but the world. No passionate profession of love for "souls" can change evil into good. These are the very sins that crucified Jesus.

It is true also that the grosser manifestations of fallen human nature are part of the kingdom of this world. Organized amusements with their emphasis upon shallow pleasure, the great empires built upon vicious and unnatural habits, unrestrained abuse of normal appetites, the artificial world called "high society"—these are all of the world. They are all part of that which is flesh, which builds upon flesh and must perish with the flesh. And from these things the Christian must flee. All these he must put behind him and in them he must have no part. Against them he must stand quietly but firmly without compromise and without fear.

So whether the world presents itself in its uglier aspects or in its subtler and more refined forms, we must recognize it for what it is and repudiate it bluntly. We *must* do this if we would walk with God in our generation as Enoch did in his. A clean break with the world is imperative.

> *Ye adulterers and adulteresses, know ye not that the friendship of the world is enmity with God? whosoever therefore will be a friend of the world is the enemy of God.* (James 4:4)

> *Love not the world, neither the things that are in the world. If any man love the world, the love of the Father is not in him. For all that is in the world, the lust of the flesh, and the lust of the eyes, and the pride of life, is not of the Father, but is of the world.* (1 John 2:15–16)

These words of God are not before us for our consideration; they are there for our obedience and we have no right to claim the title of Christian unless we follow them.

For myself, I fear any kind of religious stir among Christians that does not lead to repentance and result in a sharp separation of the believer from the world. I am suspicious of any organized revival effort that is forced to play down the hard terms of the kingdom. No matter how attractive the movement may appear, if it is not founded in righteousness and nurtured in humility it is not of God. If it exploits the flesh, it is a religious fraud and should not have the support of any God-fearing Christian. Only that is of God which honors the Spirit and prospers at the expense of the human ego. "That, according as it is written, He that glorieth, let him glory in the Lord" (1 Corinthians 1:31).

17

AFFIRMATION AND DENIAL

The notion that we enter the Christian life by an act of acceptance is true, but that is not all the truth. There is much more to it than that. Christianity involves an acceptance and a repudiation, an affirmation and a denial. And that is not only at the moment of conversion but continually thereafter day by day in all the battle of life till the great conflict is over and the Christian is home from the wars.

To live a life wholly positive is, fortunately, impossible. Were any man able to do such a thing it could be only for a moment. Living positively would be like inhaling continuously without exhaling. Aside from its being impossible, it would be fatal. Exhalation is as necessary to life as inhalation.

To accept Christ it is necessary that we reject whatever is contrary to Him. This is a fact often overlooked by eager evangelists bent on getting results. Like the salesman who talks up the good points of his product and conceals its disadvantages, the badly informed soul winner stresses the positive side of things at the expense of the negative.

Let us not be shocked by the suggestion that there are disadvantages to the life in Christ. There most certainly are. Abel was murdered, Joseph was sold into slavery, Daniel was thrown into the den of lions, Stephen was stoned to death, Paul was beheaded, and a noble army of martyrs was put to death by various painful methods down the long centuries. And where the hostility did not lead to such violence (and mostly it did not and does not), the sons of this world nevertheless managed to make it tough for the children of God in a thousand cruel ways. Everyone who has lived for Christ in a Christless world has suffered some losses and endured some pains that he could have avoided by the simple expedient of laying down his cross.

However, the pains are short and the losses inconsequential compared with the glory that will follow, "for our light affliction, which is but for a moment, worketh for us a far more exceeding and eternal weight of glory" (2 Corinthians 4:17). But while we are here among men with our sensitive hearts exposed to the chilly blasts of the unbelieving and uncomprehending world, it is imperative that we take a realistic view of things and learn how to deal with disadvantages. And it is important that we tell the whole truth to those we are endeavoring to win.

The astute Mark Twain once pointed out that some churches actually fail to gain members because they make the way too easy, and conversely the church that is hard to get into is the one that is likely to prosper numerically. The experienced missionary knows that the book or Scripture portion that is given away free will be less valued by the receiver than if a small price had been paid for it. And the higher the price, the more precious the possession.

Our Lord called men to follow Him but He never made the way look easy. Indeed one gets the distinct impression that He made it appear extremely hard. Sometimes He said things to disciples or prospective disciples that we today discreetly avoid repeating when we are trying to win men to Him. What present-day evangelist would have the courage to tell an inquirer, "If any man will come after me, let him deny himself, and take up his cross, and follow me. For whosoever will save his life shall lose it: and whosoever will lose his life for my sake shall find it" (Matthew 16:24–25)? And do not we do some tall explaining when someone asks us what Jesus meant when He said, "Think not that I am come to send peace on earth: I came not to send peace, but a sword. For I am come to set a man at variance against his father, and the daughter against her mother, and the daughter in law against her mother in law" (10:34–35)? That kind of rugged, sinewy Christianity is left for an occasional missionary or for some believer behind one of the various curtains in the world. The masses of professed Christians simply do not have the moral muscle to enable them to take a path so downright and final as this.

The contemporary moral climate does not favor a faith as tough and fibrous as that taught by our Lord and His apostles. The delicate, brittle saints being produced in our religious hot-houses today are hardly to be compared with the committed, expendable believers who once gave their witness among men. And the fault lies with our leaders. They are too timid to tell the people all the truth. They are now asking men to give to God that which costs them nothing.

Our churches these days are filled (or one-quarter filled) with a soft breed of Christian that must be fed on a diet of harmless fun to keep them interested. About theology they know little. Scarcely any of them have read even one of the great Christian classics, but most of them are familiar with religious fiction and spine-tingling films. No wonder their moral and spiritual constitution is so frail. Such can only be called weak adherents of a faith they never really understood.

When will Christians learn that to love righteousness it is necessary to hate sin? That to accept Christ it is necessary to reject self? That to follow the good way we must flee from evil? That a friend of the world is an enemy of God? That God allows no twilight zone between two altogethers where the fearful and the doubting may take refuge at once from hell to come and the rigors of present discipline?

RESISTING
THE ENEMY

S omeday the Church can relax her guard, call her watchmen down from the wall, and live in safety and peace; but not yet, not yet.

All that is good in the world stands as a target for all that is evil and manages to stay alive only by constant watchfulness and the providential protection of Almighty God. As a man or a nation may be in deepest trouble when unaware of any trouble at all and in gravest danger when ignorant that any danger exists, so the church may be in greatest peril by not recognizing the presence of peril or the source from which it comes.

The church at Laodicea has stood for nineteen hundred years as a serious warning to the whole Church of Christ to be most watchful when no enemy is in sight and to remain poor in spirit when earthly wealth increases, yet we appear to have learned nothing from her. We expound the seven letters to the churches of Asia and then return to our own company to live like the Laodicean church. There is in us a bent to backsliding that is all but impossible to cure.

The healthiest man has enough lethal bacteria in him to kill him within twenty-four hours except for one thing—the amazing power of the human organism to resist bacterial attack. Every mortal body must fight its internal enemies day and night. Once it surrenders, its hours are numbered. Quite literally it must fight or die.

The reason for this is that the human race inhabits a fallen world, which is in many ways hostile to it. Nature as well as man is fallen; and as sin is normal human powers gone astray, so disease results from microscopic creatures once meant to be useful to men but, now out of hand and perverted. To live, the body must resist these invisible enemies successfully, and considering our high vulnerability and the number of our enemies, it is wonderful that any of us manages to live beyond his childhood.

The Church lives in a hostile world. Within and around her are enemies that not only could destroy her, but are meant to and will unless she resists force with yet greater force. The Christian would collapse from sheer external pressure were there not within him a counterpressure sufficiently great to prevent it. The power of the Holy Spirit is, therefore, not optional but necessary. Without it the children of God simply cannot live the life of heaven on earth. The hindrances are too many and too effective.

A Church is a living organism and is subject to attack from such enemies as prey on living things. Yet the figure of the human body to stand for the Church is not adequate, for the life of the body is nonintelligent, whereas the Church is composed of moral beings having intelligence to recognize their enemies and a will to enable them to resist. The human body can fight its enemies even while it is asleep, but the Church cannot. She must be awake and determined or she cannot win.

One enemy we must resist is *unbelief.* The temptation is strong to reject what we cannot explain, or at least to withhold belief till we have investigated further. This attitude is proper, even commendable, for the scientist, but wholly wrong for the Christian. Here is the reason:

The faith of the Christian rests down squarely upon the man Christ Jesus who declares that He is both God and Lord. This claim must be received by pure faith or rejected outright; it can never be proved by investigation. That is why Christ's appeal is directed to faith alone. The believer thinks, it is true; but he thinks because he believes, not in order that he may. Faith secures from the indwelling Spirit confirmation exquisitely perfect, but only after it is there without other support than Christ Himself.

Another enemy is *complacency.* "Woe to them that are at ease in Zion" (Amos 6:1). The contented Christian is not in danger of attack, he has already been attacked. He is sick and does not know it. To escape this we must stir up the gift of God that is in us. We must declare war on contentment and press toward the mark for the prize of the high calling of God in Christ Jesus.

Again, there is *self-righteousness.* The temptation to feel morally pleased with ourselves will be all the greater as our lives become better. The only sure defense against this is to cultivate a quiet state of continual penitence. A sweet but sobering memory of our past guilt and a knowledge of our present imperfections are not incompatible with the joy of the Lord; and they are of inestimable aid in resisting the enemy.

The fear of man brings a snare, said the prophet, and this enemy, too, must be defeated. Our whole modern world is geared to destroy individual independence and bring all of us into conformity to all the rest of us. Any deviation from the pattern, whatever that pattern may be at the time, will not be forgiven by society, and since the Christian must deviate radically from the world, he naturally comes in for the world's displeasure. If he surrenders to fear he has been conquered, and he dare not let this happen.

Other enemies may be identified, such as *love of luxury, secret sympathy with the world, self-confidence, pride*, and *unholy thoughts*. These we must resist with every power within us, looking unto Jesus, the author and finisher of our faith.

THE WIND
IN OUR FACE

"God hath called you to Christ's side," wrote the saintly Rutherford, "and the wind is now in Christ's face in this land; and seeing ye are with Him, ye cannot expect the lee-side or the sunny side of the brae."

With that beautiful feeling for words that characterized Samuel Rutherford's most casual utterance, he here crystallizes for us one of the great radical facts of the Christian life. The wind is in Christ's face, and because we go with Him we too shall have the wind in our face. We should not expect less.

The yearning for the sunny side of the brae is natural enough, and for such sensitive creatures as we are it is, I suppose, quite excusable. No one enjoys walking into a cold wind. Yet the Church has had to march with the wind in her face through the long centuries.

In our eagerness to make converts I am afraid we have lately been guilty of using the technique of modern salesmanship, which is of course to present only the desirable qualities in a product and ignore the rest. We go to men and offer them a cozy home on the sunny side of the brae. If they will but accept Christ He will give them peace of mind, solve their problems, prosper their business, protect their families, and keep them happy all day long. They believe us and come, and the first cold wind sends them shivering to some counselor to find out what has gone wrong; and that is the last we hear of many of them.

The teachings of Christ reveal Him to be a realist in the finest meaning of that word. Nowhere in the Gospels do we find anything visionary or overoptimistic. He told His hearers the whole truth and let them make up their minds. He might grieve over the retreating form of an inquirer who could not face up to the truth, but He never ran after him to try to win him with rosy promises. He would have men follow Him, knowing the cost, or He would let them go their ways.

All this is but to say that Christ is honest. We can trust Him. He knows that He will never be popular among the sons of Adam and He knows that His followers need not expect to be. The wind that blows in His face will be felt by all who travel with Him, and we are not intellectually honest when we try to hide that fact from them.

By offering our hearers a sweetness-and-light gospel and promising every taker a place on the sunny side of the brae, we not only cruelly deceive them, we guarantee also a high casualty rate among the converts won on such terms. On certain foreign fields the expression "rice Christians" has been coined to describe those who adopt Christianity for profit. The experienced missionary knows that the convert who must pay a heavy price for his faith in Christ is the one who will persevere to the end. He begins with the wind in his face, and should the storm grow in strength he will not turn back, for he has been conditioned to endure it.

By playing down the cost of discipleship we are producing rice Christians by the tens of thousands right here on the North American continent. Old-timers will remember the Florida land boom of some years ago when a few unscrupulous real estate brokers got rich by selling big chunks of alligator swamp to innocent Northerners at fancy prices. Right now there's a boom in religious real estate on the sunny side of the brae. Thousands are investing and a few promoters are getting rich; but when the public finds out what it has bought, some of those same promoters are going out of business. And it can't happen too soon.

What has Christ to offer to us that is sound, genuine, and desirable? He offers forgiveness of sins, inward cleansing, peace with God, eternal life, the gift of the Holy Spirit, victory over temptation, resurrection from the dead, a glorified body, immortality, and a dwelling place in the house of the Lord forever. These are a few benefits that come to us as a result of faith in Christ and total committal to Him. Add to these the expanding wonders and increasing glories that shall be ours through the long, long reaches of eternity, and we get an imperfect idea of what Paul called "the unsearchable riches of Christ" (Ephesians 3:8).

To accept the call of Christ changes the returning sinner indeed, but it does not change the world. The wind still blows toward hell, and the man who is walking in the opposite direction will have the wind in his face. And we had better take this into account when we ponder on spiritual things. If the unsearchable riches of Christ are not worth suffering for, then we should know it now and cease to play at religion.

When the rich young ruler learned the cost of discipleship he went away sorrowing. He could not give up the sunny side of the brae. But thanks be to God, there are some in every age who refuse to go back. The Acts of the Apostles is the story of men and women who turned their faces into the stiff wind of persecution and loss and followed the Lamb whithersoever He went. They knew that the world hated Christ without a cause and hated them for His sake; but for the glory that was set before them they continued steadfastly on the way.

Perhaps the whole thing can be reduced to a simple matter of faith or unbelief. Faith sees afar the triumph of Christ and is willing to endure any hardship to share in it. Unbelief is not sure of anything except that it hates the wind and loves the sunny side of the brae. Every man will have to decide for himself whether or not he can afford the terrible luxury of unbelief.

THE CROSS
DOES INTERFERE

"Things have come to a pretty pass," said a famous Englishman testily, "when religion is permitted to interfere with our private lives."

To which we may reply that things have come to a worse pass when an intelligent man living in a Protestant country could make such a remark. Had this man never read the New Testament? Had he never heard of Stephen? Or Paul? Or Peter? Had he never thought about the millions who followed Christ cheerfully to violent death, sudden or lingering, because they *did* allow their religion to interfere with their private lives?

But we must leave this man to his conscience and his Judge and look into our own hearts. Maybe he but expressed openly what some of us feel secretly. Just how radically has our religion interfered with the neat pattern of our own lives? Perhaps we had better answer that question first.

I have long believed that a man who spurns the Christian

faith outright is more respected before God and the heavenly powers than the man who pretends to religion but refuses to come under its total domination. The first is an overt enemy, the second a false friend. It is the latter who will be spewed out of the mouth of Christ; and the reason is not hard to understand.

One picture of a Christian is a man carrying a cross. "If any man will come after me, let him deny himself, and take up his cross daily and follow me" (Luke 9:23). The man with a cross no longer controls his destiny; he lost control when he picked up his cross. That cross immediately became to him an all-absorbing interest, an overwhelming interference. No matter what he may desire to do, there is but one thing he *can* do; that is, move on toward the place of crucifixion.

The man who will not tolerate interference is under no compulsion to follow Christ. "If anyone would," said our Lord, and thus freed every man and placed the Christian life in the realm of voluntary choice.

Yet no man can escape interference. Law, duty, hunger, accident, natural disasters, illness, death, all intrude into his plans, and in the long run there is nothing he can do about it. Long experience with the rude necessities of life has taught men that these interferences will be thrust upon them sooner or later, so they learn to make what terms they can with the inevitable. They learn how to stay within the narrow circular rabbit path where the least interference is to be found. The bolder ones may challenge the world, enlarge the circle somewhat, and so increase the number of their problems, but no one invites trouble deliberately. Human nature is not built that way.

Truth is a glorious but hard mistress. She never consults,

bargains or compromises. She cries from the top of the high places: "Receive my instruction, and not silver; and knowledge rather than choice gold" (Proverbs 8:10). After that, every man is on his own. He may accept or refuse, receive or set at naught as he pleases; and there will be no attempt at coercion, though the man's whole destiny is at stake.

Let a man become enamored of eternal wisdom and set his heart to win her and he takes on himself a full-time, all-engaging pursuit. Thereafter he will have room for little else. Thereafter his whole life will be filled with seekings and findings, self-repudiations, tough disciplines, and daily dyings as he is being crucified unto the world and the world unto him.

Were this an unfallen world the path of truth would be a smooth and easy one. Had the nature of man not suffered a huge moral dislocation there would be no discord between the way of God and the way of man. I assume that in heaven the angels live through a thousand serene millenniums without feeling the slightest discord between their desires and the will of God. But not so among men on earth. Here the natural man receives not the things of the Spirit of God; the flesh lusts against the Spirit and the Spirit against the flesh, and these are contrary one to the other. In that contest there can be only one outcome. We must surrender and God must have His way. His glory and our eternal welfare require that it be so.

Another reason that our religion must interfere with our private lives is that we live in the world, the Bible name for human society. The regenerated man has been inwardly separated from society as Israel was separated from Egypt at the crossing of the Red Sea. The Christian is a man of heaven temporarily living on earth. Though in spirit divided from the race of fallen men he must yet in the flesh live among them. In many things he is like them, but in others he differs so radically from them that they cannot but see and resent it. From the days of Cain and Abel the man of earth has punished the man of heaven for being different. The long history of persecution and martyrdom confirms this.

But we must not get the impression that the Christian life is one continuous conflict, one unbroken irritating struggle against the world, the flesh, and the devil. A thousand times no. The heart that learns to die with Christ soon knows the blessed experience of rising with Him, and all the world's persecutions cannot still the high note of holy joy that springs up in the soul that has become the dwelling place of the Holy Spirit.

POWER REQUIRES SEPARATION

History shows clearly enough that true spirituality has never at any time been the possession of the masses. In any given period since the fall of the human race, only a few persons ever discerned the right way or walked in God's law.

God's truth has never been popular. Wherever Christianity becomes popular, it is not on its way to die—it has already died.

Popular Judaism slew the prophets and crucified Christ. Popular Christianity killed the Reformers, jailed the Quakers, and drove John Wesley into the streets. When it comes to religion, the crowds are always wrong. At any time there are a few who see, and the rest are blinded. To stand by the truth of God against the current religious vogue is always unpopular and may be downright dangerous.

The historic church, while she was a hated minority group, had a moral power that made her terrible to evil and invincible before her foes. When the Roman masses, without change of heart, were made Christian by baptism, Christianity gained popularity and lost her spiritual glow. From there she went on to adopt the ways of Rome and to follow her pagan religions. The fish caught the fisherman, and what started out to be the conversion of Rome became finally the conversion of the church. From that ignominious captivity, the church has never been fully delivered.

Christianity's scramble for popularity today is an unconscious acknowledgment of spiritual decline. Her eager fawning at the feet of the world's great is a grief to the Holy Spirit and an embarrassment to the sons of God. The lick-spittle attitude of popular Christian leaders toward the world's celebrities would make such men as Elijah or George Fox sick to the stomach.

Saving truth is a rare treasure, and not many in any generation possess it. No man ever found the way to God by asking the church member on his way to a social.

Lot was a popular believer. He sat in the gates of Sodom. But when trouble struck, he had to send quick for Abraham to get him out of the jam. And where did they find Abraham? Out on the hillside, far away from the fashionable crowds. It has always been so. For every Elijah there have always been four hundred popular prophets of Baal. For every Noah there is always a vast multitude who will not believe it is going to rain.

We are sent to bless the world, but never are we told to compromise with it. Our glory lies in a spiritual withdrawal from all that builds on dust. The bee finds no honey while crawling around the hive. Honey is in the flower far away where there is quiet and peace and the sun and the flowing stream; there the bee must go to find it. The Christian will find slim pickings where professed believers play and pray all in one breath. He may be compelled sometimes to travel alone or at least to go with the ostracized few. To belong to the despised minority may be the price he must pay for power. But power is cheap at any price.

SCIENCE AND PHILOSOPHY MORE BIGOTED THAN RELIGION

Science and philosophy are more arrogant and bigoted than religion could ever possibly be. They try to brand evangelical Christians as bigots.

But I have never taken my Bible and gone into the laboratory and tried to tell the scientist how to conduct his experiments, and I would thank him if he didn't bring his test tube into the holy place and tell me how to conduct mine!

Studying the philosophers may clarify my thinking and may help me and broaden my outlook, but it is *not* necessary to my salvation.

The scientist has nothing he can tell me about Jesus Christ, our Lord. There is nothing he can add, and I do not need to appeal to him.

I have studied Plato and the rest of them from the time I was knee-high to a rubber worker in Akron, Ohio. But I have never found that Plato added anything, finally, to what Jesus Christ has said.

Jesus said: "I am the Light that lighteth every man. I am the Bread that feedeth every man. I am the One who came from the heart of the Father, and I am the Eternal Word which was in the beginning with God, and which was and is God, and that's who I am."

So, we are assured in the Word that it is Jesus only and He is enough.

It is not Jesus PLUS a lot of other religions.

It is not Jesus PLUS a lot of other philosophies.

Jesus will never qualify or compromise anything He has said.

The honest heart that comes to Him and does not understand may need a day or a month or a year or ten years to help him prove and help him understand.

But that heart will be assured that Jesus will never change His stance. He will never, never say anything but what He said.

Never will He put in a footnote to explain, "I didn't mean it quite like that." He said what He meant—He meant what He said. He is the Eternal Word, and so we must listen to Him!

Now, what I always want to know is why did He say it, and what did He mean. A generation that knows only *what* God said will be followed by a generation that doesn't believe what God said. I am in favor of a generation of Christian thinkers—Christian philosophers, if you please—and by that, I mean that the children of God should have hold of the truth of God.

Paul spoke out against science falsely so-called, and against the vain philosophy of the world. Yet, Paul has been reckoned by men who are supposed to know as one of the six great thinkers of all time.

Paul would have cancelled himself out if he had denied the place of deep thought and of penetration and understanding in the things of God.

23

NOTHING CAN DESTROY CHRISTIANITY IF WE LIVE LIKE CHRISTIANS

I don't think communism is the great danger to Christianity. I don't believe that communism can ever destroy Christianity, if Christians will really live like Christians.

Neither do I believe that all of the liberals and modernists put together can kill Christianity. They're trying—but they can't succeed!

The atheist and the unbeliever, the pagan in his darkness—I have some understanding for these. But the liberal—he's the man who has put his own eyes out, and I haven't much sympathy for him. But he can't destroy the Christian church or the evangelical witness of Christ.

They couldn't destroy Christianity in the Roman empire. Every time they killed ten believers, one hundred others came forward and said, "Kill me, too." History tells us that.

The emperors threw so many Christians to the lions in the

pits that they began to get embarrassed, and said, "What are we going to do with these fools? We kill ten, and a hundred others stand up and confess that they are Christians, too."

So, they had to call it off. And they said, "Let's try to save face. Don't kill so many—the place is getting too bloody."

Christians were willing to live like Christians, and to die like Christians. Christian blood was the seed that made the church grow.

That's why I say that communism can never destroy the church of Jesus Christ. And you need not worry about the true church behind the Iron Curtain.

My brothers and sisters, there have been periods down through the years when Christians met in damp basements, among the flatworms and cobwebs, and worshipped their God. Then they had to sneak out to their jobs, and at night, like Gideon, went again to some hiding place and prayed and sang in a low voice, and read any portions of Scripture they could get.

They kept the fire alive in the midst of the fiercest and most brutal persecution.

THE FIRE OF GOD CAN'T BE DAMPED OUT BY THE WATERS OF MAN'S PERSECUTION

It is only when the church is rotten inside that she can die. If the church in Russia is dead today, it is not because of communism—though communism is from hell, there's no question about that—but hell can't destroy the church.

I say, if the church in Russia is dead—and I don't think it is

—it is because the institutional church had died from within.

The tree that is blown down in the storm is rotten in its heart or it wouldn't be blown down. And the church that falls because of persecution is a church that was dead before it fell.

So, I haven't much worry about communism. Neither have I much worry about liberalism.

Some of my poor, tired brethren, faint, yet pursuing, are still running after the liberals—taking a pot shot at liberals wherever they can see the white of an eye.

But I don't bother them, because they are dead, anyhow.

24

WE ARE WHAT WE ARE ANYWAY

"Let not thy peace depend on the tongues of men," said the wise old Christian mystic Thomas a Kempis; "for whether they judge well or ill, thou art not on that account other than thyself."

The desire to stand well with our fellow men is a natural one, and quite harmless up to a point, but when that desire becomes so all-consuming that we cannot be happy apart from the praises of men, it is no longer harmless, it is sinful in itself and injurious in its effects.

One of the first things a Christian should get used to is abuse. The sweetest soul ever to live in this world was subjected to an ever-increasing barrage of vile calumny during His walk among men; and if they so used the Master of the house, how can the servants hope to escape?

The only way to avoid evil tongues is to withdraw entirely from the society of men; and even then there might be those who would raise a meaningful eyebrow and suggest that perhaps after all we may have had a pretty good reason for getting under cover! To do nothing is to get abused for laziness, and to do anything is to get abused for not doing something else.

Was it not Voltaire who said that some people were like insects, they would never be noticed except that they sting? A traveler must make up his mind to go on regardless of the insects that make his trip miserable. They cannot stop a determined man; they can only make his journey unpleasant. So it is with the people who delight to swarm around the ears of God's servants as they move onward toward their appointed goal. We may all expect to be stung by our many fellow humans who appear to have dedicated themselves to the task of causing minor heartaches wherever they can as long as they can to as many people as possible. These misguided people cannot be escaped, they can only be endured.

One thing is certain, a Christian's standing before God does not depend upon his standing before men. A high reputation does not make a man dearer to God, nor does the tongue of the slanderer influence God's attitude toward His people in any way. He knows us each one, and we stand or fall in the light of His perfect knowledge.

Let us be sure that we are right with God and with men; after that there is nothing we can do except to "both hope and quietly wait for the salvation of the Lord." And by the indwelling power of the Holy Spirit, we may do our hoping and waiting in such a way that our enemies will be forced to admit that we have been with Jesus and learned of Him.

SOURCES

Chapter 1: The Sacrament of Living
A. W. Tozer, *The Pursuit of God:* (Camp Hill, PA: Christian Publications, 1948; repr. Chicago: Moody, 2015), 111–21.

Chapter 2: An Unchanging Book in an Ever-Changing World
A. W. Tozer, *Rut, Rot or Revival,* comp. James L. Snyder (Camp Hill, PA: Christian Publications,1993), 90–100.

Chapter 3: Two Portraits of the Church
Tozer, *Rut, Rot or Revival,* 102–11.

Chapter 4: The Great Test: Modifying the Truth
Tozer, *Rut, Rot or Revival,* 151–63.

Chapter 5: A Biblical Concept of the Church
Tozer, *Rut, Rot or Revival,* 113–24.

Chapter 6: A Model Church
Tozer, *Rut, Rot or Revival,* 125–38.

Chapter 7: Integration or Repudiation?
A. W. Tozer, *The Price of Neglect,* comp. Harry Verploegh (Camp Hill, PA: Christian Publications, 1991; repr. Camp Hill, PA: WingSpread, 2010), 62–64.

Chapter 8: Sure! Pay That Income Tax
A. W. Tozer, *The Early Tozer: A Word in Season,* comp. James L. Snyder (Camp Hill, PA: Christian Publications, 1997), 9–10.

Chapter 9: Measuring Spirituality by Public Prayers
Tozer, *The Early Tozer: A Word in Season,* 69–70.

Chapter 10: Wanted: Courage with Moderation
A. W. Tozer, *God Tells the Man Who Cares* (Camp Hill, PA: Christian Publications, 1993; repr. Camp Hill, PA: WingSpread, 2010), 122–27.

Chapter 11: The Honest Use of Religious Words
A. W. Tozer, *The Set of the Sail* (Camp Hill, PA: Christian Publications, 1986; repr. Camp Hill, PA: WingSpread, 2009), 157–60.

Chapter 12: The Right Attitude toward Our Spiritual Leaders
Tozer, *The Set of the Sail,* 161–64.

Chapter 13: The "Spiritual-or-Secular" Tightrope
A. W. Tozer, *Faith Beyond Reason* (Camp Hill, PA: WingSpread, 2009), 129–44.

Chapter 14: This World: Playground or Battleground?
Tozer, *God Tells the Man Who Cares,* 171–74.

Chapter 15: Are We Evangelicals Social Climbing?
A. W. Tozer, *The Warfare of the Spirit* (Camp Hill, PA: Christian Publications, 1993; repr. Camp Hill, PA: WingSpread, 2006), 13–16.

Chapter 16: Why the World Cannot Receive
A. W. Tozer, *God's Pursuit of Man* (Camp Hill, PA: Christian Publications, 1950; repr. Chicago: Moody, 2015), 115–26.

Chapter 17: Affirmation and Denial
A. W. Tozer, *That Incredible Christian* (Camp Hill, PA: Christian Publications, 1964; repr. Camp Hill, PA: WingSpread, 2008), 85–88.

Chapter 18: Resisting the Enemy
Tozer, *That Incredible Christian,* 101–4.

Chapter 19: The Wind in Our Face
Tozer, *That Incredible Christian,* 141–44.

Chapter 20: The Cross Does Interfere
A. W. Tozer, *The Radical Cross* (Camp Hill, PA: Christian Publications, 2005; repr. Chicago: Moody: 2015), 49–52.

Chapter 21: Power Requires Separation
A. W. Tozer, The Next Chapter after the Last, comp. and ed. Harry Verplough (Camp Hill, PA: Christian Publications, 1987; repr. Camp Hill, PA: WingSpread, 2010), 21–23.

Chapter 22: Science and Philosophy More Bigoted Than Religion
A. W. Tozer, *Tozer Speaks,* vol. 1, comp. Gerald R. Smith (Camp Hill, PA: Christian Publications 1994; repr. Chicago: Moody, 2010), 29–30.

Chapter 23: Nothing Can Destroy Christianity If We Live Like Christians
Tozer, *Tozer Speaks,* vol. 1, 39–41.

Chapter 24: We Are What We Are Anyway
Tozer, *The Next Chapter after the Last,* 103–5.

The Tozer Essentials

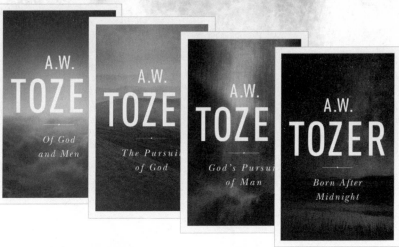

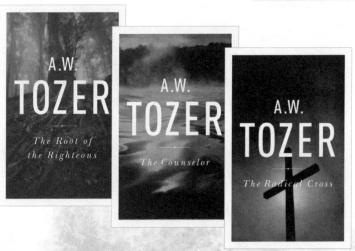

MOODY Publishers™

From the Word to Life

From the Word *to Life*

Moody Radio produces and delivers compelling programs filled with biblical insights and creative expressions of faith that help you take the next step in your relationship with Christ.

You can hear Moody Radio on 36 stations and more than 1,500 radio outlets across the U.S. and Canada. Or listen on your smartphone with the Moody Radio app!

www.moodyradio.org